A Mo
for Parents of Teens:
365 Rejuvenating Reflections

By Patricia Hoolihan

SEARCH INSTITUTE PRESS

For GARY may you FIND COMFORT & ENcouRAGEMENT IN THESE PAGES & FOR your JOURNEY!

Patricia Hoolihan

A Moment's Peace for Parents of Teens:
365 Rejuvenating Reflections
Patricia Hoolihan
Copyright © 2007
by Search Institute Press

Search Institute® and Developmental
Assets® are trademarks of Search Institute.

The contents of this book have been
reviewed by a number of parenting
professionals. Every effort has been made
to provide sound advice; however, the
information contained is not intended to
take the place of appropriate counsel or
other professional help. The publisher,
editor, and reviewers take no responsibility for the use of any of the materials or
methods described in this book, or for the
products thereof.

Quote by Dr. Elisabeth Kübler-Ross
reprinted by permission of the EKR
Foundation (www.ekrfoundation.org and
www.elisabethkublerross.com).

Quotes by Michael Riera, Ph.D., are
reprinted from *Staying Connected to Your
Teenager: How to Keep Them Talking
to You and How to Hear What They're
Really Saying* by Michael Riera, Ph.D.,
© 2003, Da Capo Press of the Perseus
Books Group.

10 9 8 7 6 5 4 3 2 1

Printed on acid-free paper in
the United States of America.

Search Institute
615 First Avenue Northeast, Suite 125
Minneapolis, MN 55413
www.search-institute.org
www.mvparents.com
612-376-8955 • 800-888-7828

Credits
Editors: Anitra Budd, Susan Wootten
Cover design: Percolator
Interior design: Prism Publishing Center
Production Coordinator: Mary Ellen
        Buscher
Reviewers: Mike Diamanti, Kristin
        Green, Taryn Gemelke, Tenessa
        Gemelke, Doug Hoffacker, Patricia
        Howell-Blackmore, Leah Shrum,
        Claudia Hoffacker, Paul Kirst,
        Michael Pittman

**Library of Congress Cataloging-in-
Publication Data**

Hoolihan, Patricia.
  A moment's peace for parents of teens :
365 rejuvenating reflections / by Patricia
Hoolihan.
    p.   cm.
  Summary: "This resource offers
daily meditations for parents of teens.
Inspiration, insight, and comfort are
readily available in short, daily doses. The
philosophy that raising a child is not a
one-way street from parent to child, but
is a flowing interaction between parent
and child, and among all family members;
focusing on a child's strengths and
talents is a way to help parents see their
parenting paths more clearly"--Provided
by publisher.
  ISBN-13: 978-1-57482-247-2 (pbk. : alk.
paper)
  ISBN-10: 1-57482-247-0 (pbk. : alk.
paper)
  1. Parenting. 2. Parent and teenager.
3. Affirmations. I. Title.

HQ755.8.H653 2007
649'.125--dc22

                    2006037303

Contents

Acknowledgments

Thanks, first and foremost, to Search Institute for giving me the opportunity to write this book. Many thanks to Anitra Budd, my editor, whose sharp eye fine-tuned much of this material.

Several books that have been written on adolescents were invaluable to me for their sensitivity and wisdom. These books are: *WHY Do They Act That Way?: A Survival Guide to the Adolescent Brain for You and Your Teen*, by David Walsh, Ph.D.; *Get Out of My Life, but First Could You Drive Me and Cheryl to the Mall?: A Parent's Guide to the New Teenager*, by Anthony E. Wolf, Ph.D.; *A Parent's Guide to the Teen Years: Raising Your 11- to 14-Year-Old in the Age of Chat Rooms and Navel Rings*, by Susan Panzarine; and *Staying Connected to Your Teenager: How to Keep Them Talking to You and How to Hear What They're Really Saying*, by Michael Riera, Ph.D. These books were extremely helpful to me in the writing of these pages and in thinking about relating to my teens.

As always, I owe a debt of gratitude to my friends and fellow travelers on this parenting journey. Deep thanks to all the parents of the friends of my children, invaluable partners—especially Marti and John, Christine and Todd, Jane and Steve, Mary and Wally, Margaret and David, and many others too numerous to name. Each of your children brings a special light to our family life: thank you.

Where would I be without my running friends? For stories, shared dilemmas, books, endless advice, and the deep well of sanity provided through friendship and getting out around the lake every day, thanks go to Mary Reyelts, Beth Dooley, Leslie Bush, Marti Hickner, Kate Ellis, Angie Lillehei, and Randy Lebedoff.

A special thanks to all my friends, even if you aren't named here. You all inspire me, each in your own way.

Many thanks to my siblings and in-laws for modeling and sharing the parenting of teens and for my wonderful nieces and nephews.

Thanks always and forever to my husband, who teaches teenagers and who inspires me as I watch how he can talk to any teenager anywhere at any time: truly a gift.

And, of course, thanks to Caitlin and Kelly. You're the best!

Introduction

Search Institute asked me to write this book and I can't thank them enough for doing so. The timing was so right for me, the topic so close to my heart. I have been parenting a teenager since I married my husband and became a stepmom more than twenty years ago. We now have two teenagers between us.

This book is not so much a survival guide as a companion, a quiet place to help you remember you are not alone on this journey of parenting a teen. Each day's entry opens with a quotation, then a short reflection on the topic of the day and then a closing thought or suggested activity for the day.

A wide range of topics and issues are covered here, such as coping with teen substance abuse, the importance of careful listening, and enjoying funny moments with your child, but perhaps the overarching theme is a reminder of the real issues abounding in this age group that parents have to wrestle with. There is permission here for self-acceptance and self-nurturing, permission to be a good parent without expecting to be a perfect parent, and permission to understand rather than judge yourself and your teen.

I found my own parenting becoming more intentional as I immersed myself in researching and writing this book, and I hope reading it does the same for you.

I also hope each day's reflection is a source of inspiration, comfort, or courage. It's not an easy journey, parenting this age group; each child holds particular challenges and special gifts. As we meet the challenges, hopefully we are more able to cherish the gifts. These daily thoughts are meant to encourage and sustain you, the parent. You are a very important guide for your child through this passage of her or his life. Happy navigating to you.

January 1

A holiday gives one a chance to look backward and forward, to reset oneself by an inner compass.

– May Sarton

There is a deep internal wisdom built into the calendar that has been created over long periods of time. There's an alternating rhythm between work/school days and the weekend. There are periodic holidays and long weekends that provide breaks everyone looks forward to.

Whether a holiday is one day outside of the usual schedule or a week or two away, it provides the benefit of a change of pace and thus a change in perception. A break from routine offers a great opportunity to see things more clearly and objectively.

I will honor the holiday, here or coming up, by using it as a chance to reflect on my life and the life of my child.

January 2

In automobile terms, the child supplies the power but the parents have to do the steering.

— Dr. Benjamin Spock

How much or how little impact we have on our children's lives is a delicate and ever-changing balance. To a great extent they drive their own destinies. It is their interests and their energy levels and their goals that primarily make up who they are. But parents are key to steering children down the roads of opportunity. Parents provide important guidelines, marking the guardrails on the road of life.

Just like a toddler needs to be redirected at times, so do teenagers. Sometimes you need to remind them of the speed limit. Sometimes it's helpful to point out another, less traveled path. And of course the more subtle the steering, the more effective.

I will look around today and see where my child might need some quiet but firm steering.

January 3

*Know the golden mean in what one can
expect and what is just too much.*

·- Doris Bodmer

Parents' expectations of teens can be a sticky issue, demanding careful thought. It helps to be aware of your own expectations. Identify what's best for your teen, noting her individual needs and gifts, and pay attention to times when your agenda gets in the way. Earning an "A" in English might be an attainable goal for a teen who's already doing well, but expecting it from a teen who's failing can cause enormous stress and frustration for you both. Work with your teen to create reasonable expectations, perhaps aiming for a "C" instead of a perfect mark.

What's your bottom line? When are you asking too much? These are important questions to consider. And when you realize you might be demanding too much, you can back off. Reassess. Reroute yourself. Responsive expectations are often more meaningful than rigid ones.

If I bump up against the wall of my own rigidity, I will take time to be thoughtful about what I'm asking for and why. Clarity of purpose is my goal today.

January 4

Soon silence will have passed into legend.
Man has turned his back on silence. Day
after day he invents machines and devices
that increase noise and distract human-
ity from the essence of life, contemplation,
meditation.

— Jean Arp

I was once lucky enough to interview several nuns for a photo-essay project. There was something about the serenity and joy and focus of their lives that touched me deeply. They set aside time every day for reflection, as well as large blocks of time at regular intervals throughout the year. Listening time, they often called it—spiritual listening.

If we as parents devoted even a fraction of this kind of time to reflection, meditation, and listening, we would feel the benefits. There are many words for it, this process that is essentially about slowing down and taking time to be thoughtful. Time to think about what our intentions are as parents. Such thinking time is the beginning of fruitful action.

What is it I want to be intentional about as a parent right now? I'll take time to think about this today.

January 5

Treat yourself with gentle care.
— William Martin

The job of parenting—especially teens—can be a rigorous, demanding, sleep-depriving, and ego-bruising experience. Keeping up with the energy and needs of a teenager is not for the faint of heart.

It is much harder if we allow ourselves to be too worn down, and if we don't take time to rejuvenate our own energies. It is essential to remember to treat ourselves with gentleness—to not be too hard on ourselves when we make mistakes, for instance. Unfortunately, teens can be very hard on us, and we need to balance that out. We all need people who can gently support us in this hard job, and we all need ways to keep renewing our own energy.

Today I will be gentle with myself—I might need to forgive myself, talk with a good friend, or go on a walk.

January 6

Keep your eyes on the prize.

— Alice Wine

Teens who feel they have a purpose or a goal are teens who tend to do better in all areas of their lives. As parents, we can encourage our teens to talk about, write about, and think about what their goals are. Or we can pay attention when they talk to friends about what they want or what they are working toward. And we can ask them what some of their dreams and hopes are for the near and far future.

If kids are aware of the big picture of their lives, they tend to make more positive choices in the moment. We can help them keep their eyes on their potential by talking about and knowing their goals.

I will do all I can today to help my teen keep her or his eyes on the prize.

January 7

Your precious ones need a healthy dose of goodness, from you, daily.

— Esther Davis-Thompson

Goodness, from a parent, can come in a variety of forms: interest in a teen's day, listening, enthusiasm, gentleness, and just being there. "Good energy" is what it all boils down to. A dose of positive feelings every day is like a golden thread connecting parent and child.

Even if our teens don't seem to notice, or shrug it off, this daily dose is important and worth paying attention to. It builds slowly, a little bit every day, the weaving of golden thread, the knowledge that one is loved and appreciated.

Have I given my daily dose of goodness to my child yet today? If not, I will do so now.

January 8

*Some of the nicest friendships my teens have
are with a parent of one of their peers.*
— Kathleen Kimball-Baker

We fondly call my daughter's best friends, who live
up the street, our adopted daughters. We refer to
my son's best friend, who also lives nearby, as our
adopted son. These neighbors have taken our children on trips, fed them meals, and always welcomed
them into their homes. We attend the concerts and
plays of our friends' and neighbors' children and they
do the same.

I can see how my daughter and son are strengthened by this practice. Here are more caring adults
who want them to do their best, who appreciate
their talents, who enjoy their company, and who
help make them stronger people and their world a
more loving place.

*To celebrate these relationships, I will have my teen's
friends and parents over to dinner.*

January 9

Teenagers, for better and worse, are some of
the most creative and fun people on the planet.
— Dr. Michael Riera

Recently I helped co-host a cast party for a play my
son was involved in. Although I kept myself low-
key, mostly serving food and replenishing drinks,
I was struck by what a wonderful and fun-loving
group this was. Someone was banging out tunes
on the piano, completely by ear, with others wan-
dering in and out to sing along. Laughter, affection,
and an easy cheerfulness overflowed in the room.
Occasionally someone would settle onto a stool in
the food area and chat with me.

I was struck by this delightful group of human
beings. The energy in the air was contagious and I
felt lucky to be there. I also felt inspired and hopeful.

I will do one thing this week to honor and connect with
the creative and energetic part of my teenager.

January 10

Worry often gives a small thing a big shadow.
— Swedish proverb

Worry begins with the same first letter as "waste." For something we all easily slide into, worry has never done anything but waste time and energy. It has never solved or prevented a problem. It has never been part of a solution. Yet it consumes an enormous amount of thinking time.

Whatever your worries are about yourself, your world, or your teenager, write them down and then burn them. Talk them over with a friend and then let them fly away with the wind. Don't hang on. Even if you can't stop the worries from entering your brain, you can let them go. Consciously. Easily. Into their place might come joy, contentment, and trust that things will all work out.

Today I can find a way to exchange my worry for something much more positive.

January 11

Where is home? Home is where the heart can laugh without shyness. Home is where the heart's tears can dry at their own pace.
            ~ Vernon G. Baker

Many of our teens have days or phases when they would rather be at someone else's home. But even in these phases, it's good to notice and reinforce where they gather comfort in our own homes. Perhaps it's in their bedroom, where they are surrounded by favorite books and things. Perhaps there's a room that's a special hangout for your teen, alone or with friends.

Ideally somewhere in our homes (or everywhere in our homes) makes our teens feel like they can be themselves and reach for comfort when needed.

Today I will highlight and make use of where and how my teen finds comfort in our home.

January 12

Count your blessings, not your crosses.
Count your gains, not your losses. . . .
Count your health, not your wealth.

— Irish blessing

A friend of mine found out her daughter was shoplifting. She was horrified, of course, but just a few weeks before that she had found a wonderful therapist for herself who was willing to work with both of them. She also had a friend who struggled with a similar problem and provided an especially consoling ear and several helpful books. Blessings lightened the heaviness of the experience every day.

When my parents were raising eight children and money was tight, my mother would often say, "But we are so blessed because we are all healthy." I appreciated her lack of self-pity and optimistic outlook then—and I appreciate both even more so now that I am a parent myself.

Even if I'm going through a hard time, I can look around and count the blessings coming my way.

January 13

Compassion brings us to a stop, and for a moment we rise above ourselves.

·— Mason Cooley

We parents are busy. Our kids are busy. We have expectations of them, and we're trying to make those expectations clear to help them be successful. Sometimes what is lost in all our doing is taking the time to feel compassion for our kids.

Whether preteens or teens, we can bet our children are juggling studies, friendship challenges, peer pressure, and many decisions about a number of personal values and questions. Take time to talk about all they are balancing and especially to tell them you understand how hard they're working.

I will take some time today to feel and express compassion for all my child is going through right now.

January 14

I began to see that hope, however feeble its apparent foundation, bespeaks allegiance to every unlikely beauty that remains intact on earth.

·- David James Duncan

As parents of teens we need an ever-ready source of hope. It's so easy to lose steam, so easy to worry about the holes in our children's development. Where do we turn when we are feeling low on hope or in need of it?

There is something both inspiring and comforting about the natural world's beauty. It is simply there, waiting for us. Each day brings new gifts, new demonstrations of beauty, and yet some of it is timeless beauty. It is nature's constancy that is reassuring and its brilliant, ever-renewing creative energy that can inspire us.

When I am feeling low, I can take a walk and let nature's beauty reconnect me, deeply, to hope.

January 15

The giving of love is an education in itself.
— Eleanor Roosevelt

When we signed on for the job of parent, many of us had no idea how much we had to learn. How little we could see of the ways parenting would humble us, challenge us, and bring to the surface parts of ourselves we'd rather keep hidden. Little did we know the depths of grief or valleys of disappointment ahead of us, nor the many moments of joy and satisfaction.

We signed on for the journey of love. To love children through all of their stages, and perhaps especially through their teenage years, is a deep and intense education. What we learn about ourselves, and about the world they are growing into, enriches us in ways we cannot count.

Today I will be thankful for how my teen forces me to know myself (and the world around me) better.

January 16

The greatest part of our happiness depends
on our dispositions, not our circumstances.
— Martha Washington

The dual job of being a human being and a parent is demanding. There are bound to be ups and downs, waiting periods, doubts and fears, and triumphs all along both of these paths. The key to your happiness, as a person and as a parent, is your disposition—how you see and deal with what comes your way.

Hard stuff cannot really be ignored, but it can be talked about and then let go of. It's the hanging onto the hard stuff, the focusing on it beyond its time, that weighs us down. Letting go of what's hard can be outshone by an awareness of what is right and good in our lives. A strong focus in this direction helps appreciation and gratitude easily bubble to the surface. And the basically happy, grateful disposition paves the way toward a happier life in general and throws misery overboard.

I can choose a happy, grateful disposition today.

January 17

Friendships multiply joys and divide griefs.
— H. G. Bohn

The family is a classroom for friendship. Although family has the added bonus and complication of having been born or adopted into each of our lives, it is the ability to share joys and divide griefs that is ultimately a lesson in friendship as well as family.

These lessons of loyalty and love are what teens take into their world of friendships. If they have learned at home how to be supportive when it's needed, and how to share time and fun, then these are skills they will take into their friendships. Also, as parents, our own friendships are powerful models for our teens to learn from.

I can pay attention today to how we model the sharing of joys and burdens in our family.

January 18

*And thus, like the wounded oyster, he mends
his shell with pearl.*

-- Ralph Waldo Emerson

Our own wounds and our children's wounds are
often sources of grief. If someone in the family has
struggled with chemical dependency, everyone is
touched by this. If someone in the family is grappling
with a mental illness, everyone is affected. Whatever
problems might exist in your family, there is no way
to fully protect your children from them.

What we need to remember is that this is the
fabric of real life. Every family, at one time or another, struggles with something. But it is these very
wounds that can shape our children into compassionate, empathetic, and vibrant human beings. Like
the wounded oyster that creates a pearl of beauty in
response to its wound, we can watch our children
take steps of courage and healing that will shape them
into incredible human beings.

*Today I will honor the beauty—hard-earned as it is—
that comes from mending wounds.*

January 19

Your only obligation in any lifetime is to be true to yourself.

- Richard Bach

Each of us follows a unique path, and the same is true of our children. Children try out and explore their interests and talents. As adults we have tested many more of ours, but we also sometimes move into new periods of exploration as well. Being true to ourselves requires a certain amount of reflection and clarity. It also requires our not letting the culture around us and the expectations of others inhibit us too much.

We can say we want our children to "be themselves," but it can be hard sometimes to let that happen. We may not approve of every phase they go through. We have to decide when behavior we don't like is harmless exploration or destructive enough to require intervention. Short of that, it's always good to encourage them to be who they are as individuals, to find ways to stoke the fires of their passions—ours as well.

When I veer off-course worrying about what others think, I can get back on the track of being true to myself and respecting that in my child.

January 20

How do we know when alcohol or drug use is a problem? Heredity cannot be overemphasized.

~ Mary Pipher

If addiction issues are present in our families, it is important to talk with our teens about their risk factors. They need to be gently reminded of this reality, preferably not hammered with it. This is a tricky issue, and many of us parents will have different ways of dealing with potential problems.

We can never go wrong giving our kids information about their genetic code. It is our job to pay attention to these issues. Are they drinking or experimenting with drugs? If so, under what circumstances, and for what purpose? What can we do to help them deal with this issue, which is, no matter how we would like to wish it away, a relevant one?

This week I will visit this important topic again, first by clarifying my thoughts on the issue and then by talking with my teen.

January 21

AUDIENCE MEMBER: *Do you have advice for parents?*

DALAI LAMA: *No. (laughter) It is a very hard job, very hard job.*

I was in the audience on the night of this exchange and my friends and I all laughed and nodded knowingly at each other. There was something so disarming and truthful about this wise man's response.

Who among us doesn't want magical words of advice from time to time? On the days you have no answers to your questions about your child and about yourself as a parent, remember the Dalai Lama. The job was too hard even for him to take on. His lighthearted laughter echoes in my memory, reminding me that I'm part of a centuries-old labor of love, and some days the job just has no easy answer—for any of us.

With a lighthearted attitude, I can calmly face the unknowns in my life as a parent and live today fully, even with unanswered questions.

January 22

The real art of conversation is not only to say the right thing in the right place, but, more difficult still, to leave unsaid the wrong thing at the tempting moment.

~ Dorothy Neville

Most of us have said the wrong thing at one time or another. Despite these lapses, we can learn from past mistakes and get better in this area. The wrong yet tempting things to say are often along the lines of "I told you so," or a comment that judges your teen's behavior or that of a friend, or launching into a lecture. As soon as you start, you can see it's going nowhere.

The payoff can be huge for holding back at such moments. This allows your child space: space to draw her or his own conclusions, space to talk about what is going on. It is much more fruitful and lasting if a teen comes to her or his own awarenesses. Listening to your child is such an important part of learning who she or he is.

Let me listen today, rather than saying the wrong thing.

January 23

Don't laugh at a youth for his affectations;
he is only trying on one face after another to
find his own.

– Logan Pearsall Smith

Our children will go through many phases as they navigate through the teen years, and often this involves trying on new clothing, hairstyles, attitudes, or speech patterns. We all have different limits for bared skin or for what's appropriate to wear to specific places. But beyond that, as parents we share a need to understand the journey of self-expression our kids are taking.

It's a generational truth that parents will be mystified by some of what their children will try on. It's a delicate process on our part: how much to mirror back what we see and how much to simply let go. That they are trying to figure out and express who they are is appropriate; we can have empathy for this complex process.

Even if I don't understand my child's choices, I can understand that he or she is experimenting with the necessary search for self-expression.

January 24

Focus discipline as a way to teach, not as a form of punishment.

> — *What Kids Need to Succeed: Proven, Practical Ways to Raise Good Kids*

There is an important distinction here. When we feel the impulse to punish, it usually means we are acting out of anger. Our children are going to make us angry at times, but it is important to think out consequences for behavior separately from our anger. Anger is often extreme and punitive.

It's always beneficial to think about what we want our children to learn. Consider what lesson needs to be taught here. For example, when you suspend a child's driving privileges for driving unsafely, he or she will most likely learn that those privileges must be earned.

When I am angry with my children, I can cool down and think through which consequences would teach them most effectively.

January 25

Oh, what a tangled web do parents weave
When they think that their children are naive.

∽ Ogden Nash

It's often hard to imagine our children as being the bearers of information about the intricate and difficult things in this world. But for the most part they know more than we think they do about sex, drugs, and violence. Even so, it is important for us to talk with them about these issues, these realities of life in our world today.

As awkward as it sometimes is, it's vital that children hear their parents' values and perspectives. Such conversations provide children with a chance to ask questions or to bring up any concerns they have. Most teens are making choices, and watching people around them make choices, in some or all of these areas. Most likely they see and hear more than we can (or really want to) imagine.

I will not underestimate what my child is exposed to: my voice and listening ear as a parent are important.

January 26

*Nine-tenths of wisdom is appreciation. Go
find somebody's hand and squeeze it while
there's time.*

— Dale Dauten

On the parenting road there are many people to appreciate. Teachers are often people who give kids a boost when they most need it, or see a special gift or talent in a child and help draw it out into the world. Sometimes it's a relative who says the right thing at the needed moment or who supports your child in a special way.

There are people who help us parents do our job. Perhaps it's our friends or our own parents who encourage us. It might be a wise neighbor or a professional in a time of crisis. What deepens us is taking time to be grateful to these helpers and to express that gratitude. Gratitude opens and widens the rivers of our wise hearts.

I will look around today at whom I want to thank and will take time to do so.

January 27

Like snowflakes, the human pattern is never cast twice. We are uncommonly and marvelously intricate in thought and action.

— Alice Childress

A neighbor told me once that he and his wife had several children because he finds children so interesting. Now of course there are many reasons for such a choice, but I was struck by this and I've found it instructive. When I keep this idea in mind, it serves as a reminder to look at my teenage children and remember them as interesting people.

As parents, it is good to regularly take a moment to ponder, "What is it about my son or daughter that is so wonderfully unique?" Usually there are many things, but it takes a certain awareness to heighten our focus. It is our child's uniqueness that makes parenting fun and interesting. As teenagers, they are becoming even more fascinating as they grow and develop their interests.

Today I will appreciate the uniqueness of my teen and celebrate the color and interest he or she brings to my life.

January 28

Challenge me to succeed.
— Search Institute survey respondent

Once in a while it's a good idea to ask your teen who they admire, who they would like to emulate, and who is a hero in their eyes (whether in the family, the neighborhood, or the larger world). Such a role model helps them claim ideals and goals. This exercise can be a helpful way for young people to articulate their values.

Once a goal is clarified, you and your teen can both identify potential steps toward that goal. My son admires his track coach, and every time my son is disciplined and thoughtful about how he treats his body, he is emulating his coach's value of self-respect. My son is also learning that it feels good, physically and emotionally, to strive for goals in this area of his life.

Today I will think about and honor a goal my teenager has and the steps he or she is taking (or may yet need to take) toward that goal.

January 29

Parents are the bones on which children sharpen their teeth.

— Peter Ustinov

Think for a minute about how animals need sharp teeth in order to survive in the wilderness: without them they would not be able to feed or protect themselves. Our children are developing survival skills. Our teens, especially the older ones, will soon be out in the world, out in that wilderness. They will need to know how to protect and feed themselves.

We are the bones upon which they sharpen these necessary skills. Of course we often feel chewed on, chewed up, or chewed out. Independence is hard-earned, both in the learning and in the teaching.

When I have that chewed-up feeling, I will think about what survival skill my teenager is striving to learn today.

January 30

*It is better to know some of the questions
than all of the answers.*

-- James Thurber

Sometimes parents get caught up in thinking we
should have all the answers. We think we should be
equipped at all times with clever words of wisdom
or the perfect advice at the perfect moment. Or, we
think we should know what the best choice is for
dealing with our teenager.

But life is often a weighing of options, of pros and
cons. Much of life is lived in the many degrees between clear-cut decisions. So, if we or our teenagers
are wrestling with an issue, it may be time to respect
the questions, clearly lay out the issues, and name the
pros and cons for potential, possible answers. This
process requires patience, but it is an important part
of the journey toward clarity.

*Today I will respect the questions that are present in my
life and my teenager's life.*

January 31

*A problem with giving too much of oneself
to a teenager is that if she does not pay
you back—and often adolescents do not—
a parent can feel very hurt.*

— Dr. Anthony E. Wolf

Sometimes you may find yourself giving your teen too much or too little, emotionally and materially, before you get it just right. How much you give will depend on what you're going through and the stage your teen is in.

Feeling taken advantage of by your child can be a clear sign you're giving too much. No child was ever fatally wounded by hearing the word "no"; yet we hurt *ourselves* when we continually feel like their victims. We also run the risk of harming our child's growing independence. If we meet our teen's every demand for money or rides, how will she ever learn to meet those needs on her own? Ultimately, we damage the love between parent and child when we give until it hurts.

I will protect the love I have for my child by setting appropriate boundaries when I notice I'm feeling overly hurt or mad.

February 1

The most good you can do for yourself spiritually is to play your role as parent with total love, conviction, and purpose.

— Deepak Chopra

What is best for our children is often what is good for us as well, and, conversely, what is good for us is often what is best for them. At a spiritual level, the job of caring for our children deepens and nourishes us.

Loving with conviction and purpose day after day includes a multitude of caring gestures—everything from making lunches to providing a listening ear. This practice, this spiritual discipline, will take many forms over the years. But above all, our hearts and spirits are being stretched. As we help our children reach for the stars, we get to remember the night sky.

Today I will reflect upon the ways I love my teen with a total heart and sense of purpose. Then I will name the ways this has shaped me.

February 2

If we want to influence a change in our child's behavior, we need to watch our own. Is what we are doing bringing the desired results, or are we merely brushing aside an annoyance?
— Dr. Rudolf Dreikurs

Desired results—they're key to shaping our parenting behaviors. Do we give in because it's the right thing to do? Or are we worn down against our better judgment? What is our desired goal?

Perhaps your teen complains daily about a particular teacher. It's easy to half-listen, murmur, "That's too bad," and allow him to drop the class. While it requires more of you, it's worthwhile to help your teen resolve conflicts between himself and someone with whom he disagrees or dislikes. Set up a coping strategy, or ask your teen to meet with his teacher or counselor. Initiate a phone call or e-mail, if it seems like the right step. In the long term, your teen's learning will often require your extra effort, but it's *always* worth your time.

What do I want to teach my teen today? What are the best actions I can take in order to do so?

February 3

Whatever you are holding in your heart will come directly out through your eyes when you look at your child.

·– Esther Davis-Thompson

We all struggle with negative emotions from time to time. And when we do, it's important to have ways to cleanse ourselves. Awareness, of course, is the first step, followed by action. Whether we write in a journal, meditate, talk to a counselor, or chat with a good friend, there are ways to work through feelings like resentment, anger, and bitterness.

Clearing our minds of negative emotions allows us to reenter a space of love. This is the window through which we want to view our children. Most of us do not want to pass on toxic feelings. As parents, our job is to regularly cleanse our hearts.

Today I will pay attention to where I may need to do emotional housecleaning, so I can more clearly love myself and my child.

February 4

*Teens . . . are fascinating. . . . They're fun,
irreverent and see things from a refreshingly
different perspective. Enjoy them!*

 — Dr. Susan Panzarine

Without meaning to, we sometimes forget to enjoy
these teens who live with us. We become focused
on the busy demands of our lives, on what we think
we need to do as parents, but simply enjoying them
and their friends is an essential part of being an affectionate and loving parent.

This can happen in simple ways: "hanging out"
together, cooking, biking, watching a favorite TV
show, enjoying laughter and conversation at mealtime. Sometimes car rides are good for this, both
long and short trips, or an outing together to a con-
cert or a movie.

*My time with my child is short, and I want to enjoy as
much of her or his daily presence in my life as I can.*

February 5

What ordinary thing can you do together today?

— William Martin

The key to connecting with our children is very simple—it's the act of being together. Even the simplest of ways counts and helps feed the connection. Driving in the car can be a very easy, often necessary, and surprisingly fruitful way to interact. We may groan about organizing our lives around car pools, but listening to our teens and their friends in conversation can open a door into their world.

Other ordinary ways to connect might include walking the dog together, having a short chat while you fix them a snack, or taking a trip together to the drug store to buy supplies for a school project.

I will take time to do something simple with my child today.

February 6

*We love those people who give with humility,
or who accept with ease.*

~ Freya Stark

Even though it feels like we do a lot of giving, it's good to remember how much our children love us in return. When my teenager calls me for the third time in one morning and I want to roll my eyes, I remember that she's connecting with me. When my son encourages me to do something I've wanted to do, I realize I should not be surprised to find support coming from this direction.

Even in the often-unbalanced relationship of parent and child, our children give things back to us. All we need to do is let them—and let their love and affection into our hearts.

Today I will notice and be grateful for the ways my child gives me love and encouragement.

February 7

The ideal of the self-sufficient American family is a myth. . . . Families needing one or another kind of help are not morally deficient; most families do need assistance at one time or another.

— Joseph Featherstone

Is your teen often in trouble at school or at home? Are drugs or drinking becoming an issue? Most of us as parents will have worries and concerns about our children at some point. Some of these troubles are normal and some are worthy of ongoing reflection, then action.

Fortunately, these are not issues we have to figure out all on our own. There are books, counselors, support groups, and experienced professionals all around us. All we have to do is start asking.

Many forms of kindness and help are available to me. All I have to do is reach out and ask for them.

February 8

Eighty percent of success is showing up.

~ Woody Allen

Perhaps 80 percent of parenting is showing up for kids, whether it's at their events, in their moments of crisis, or for family dinner. Showing up is the common denominator of being there—it's the beginning point of all else.

It's helpful to show up at your teen's school. It gives you a sense of what his or her life is like there. The same is true of choir concerts, plays, or sporting events. Studies show that something as simple as shared family dinners tightens and toughens the bond between parent and child.

What in my teen's life might I need to simply show up for today?

February 9

*It is important to remember that it is the
minor disappointments and discomforts that
help us build up a tolerance for the normal
pains of life.*

-- Janice Presser

Nothing is harder than watching a child suffer,
whether in small or large ways. Yet to provide a life
free of pain (even if it were possible) would be to
ill-prepare our children for life on their own. We
cannot protect them from disappointment, but we
can be there to support them through it. In this
way, the difficult moment becomes an opportunity
for learning an important life-long coping skill: one
doesn't have to be alone in hard times.

As you support your child through hard times, remember that this is an important part of the training
ground for adulthood. Instead of fighting this reality,
you can accept and embrace what is being learned.

*Today I can reflect on what my teen has the potential
to learn in challenging situations.*

February 10

If you want to know what is on your child's mind, you don't necessarily need to ask directly. Just talk with him.
— Dr. Louise Bates Ames and Dr. Frances Ilg

There have been more phone-calls or instant messages from your teenager than usual. You sense something is going on, but it's hard to tell for sure. This is a good time to volunteer to drive your teen somewhere, or to fix a favorite snack and be available for a chat in your home's hangout spot.

Small talk can open the door to larger topics. Often the casual approach to discussions works better than direct questioning. If you can create a conversational atmosphere, rather than a sense of digging for information, a teen will feel more like talking. It's all the small conversations between parents and teens that build a bridge for the more difficult conversations.

Today I will start a conversation with my teen and be open to wherever it takes us.

February 11

*The better we feel about ourselves, the fewer
times we have to knock somebody else down
to feel tall.*

— Odetta

Often, when we find ourselves criticizing others, it
means there is something going on inside us that
needs attention. It's a common human trait to try to
buck ourselves up—as people and as parents—by
putting someone else down. It's easy to be critical of
another's parenting style or of what's going on with
another child.

Feeling insecure and being unaware of it can be a
self-destructive combination. If something difficult
is going on with us, then facing it, writing about it,
or talking about it will help alleviate the need to pull
someone else down.

*When I feel myself wanting to criticize, I can instead
look deeper within. I can find more positive ways to
make myself feel better.*

February 12

From your parents you learn love and laughter and how to put one foot before the other. But when books are opened you discover that you have wings.

·- Helen Hayes

A real asset we can pass on and instill in our children is a love of learning. It is in learning, through books and schooling, that the larger world becomes open and accessible to our teens. They can depart from the grounded homebase they know well and fly off to explore other places, times, and ways of being.

We encourage our teens as students by paying attention to how and what they are doing, and by appreciating their efforts. We encourage them as learners by nurturing a love of reading and supporting their natural curiosity about the world around them.

Today I will honor my teenager's wings by honoring who he or she is as a learner.

February 13

*Music is the way that our memories sing to
us across time.*

— Lance Morrow

Most of us have strong memories connected to music.
An oldies song plays on the radio and we are trans-
ported in time to a poignant era in our lives, back to
a certain mood or significant person from the past.
Music entwines itself around our heart's and mind's
memory paths.

Keeping in mind our own musical memories, we
can notice and appreciate the music our children are
listening to, inside their headphones, on their iPods,
or as they exchange CDs or song downloads. Yes,
there's always the hazard of their being exposed to
overly obscene or violent lyrics. But aside from that
risk, music is an important and, for the most part,
positive and formative part of our teenagers' lives.

*Today I can appreciate and learn from my teen's musi-
cal interests.*

February 14

The greatest disease in the West today is not TB or leprosy; it is being unwanted, unloved and uncared for.

— Mother Teresa

If we want, love, and care for our children, we are doing a lot. These are the essentials: the big picture that is created by daily small gestures. It's easy to miss the importance of the big picture, especially when we feel worn down by the multitude of necessary small gestures of caring. Completing the big picture requires a faith in the small moments, in the ordinary demands of today.

Many children in this world do not feel wanted, loved, or cared for—perhaps one or more of those children is in our own orbit, and hungry for any gesture of kindness we can send them.

Today I will reflect on one simple but concrete way that I love my teen.

February 15

For those who have never raised a teenage child, it is hard to imagine the day-to-day swings between crazed frenzy and genuine tranquility.

— Dr. Anthony E. Wolf

When it comes to teenagers, small things can become major crises so quickly it will make your head spin. And, once you get geared up for the crisis, you might easily discover that your child now sees that crisis as no big deal.

It's as if your job as a parent is to keep a steady beat, to help in the crisis but not overreact to it. Then, when the calm returns, you're more able to receive and appreciate it. Of course it is easier to provide a steady beat if you're not overtired or overstressed yourself.

I will take a look at the last week and see where I've been successful in providing a steady beat. If I haven't been so good, I will make it a priority to steady myself more.

February 16

Angels can fly because they take themselves lightly.

> — G. K. Chesterton

Once in a while we need to lighten our load simply by taking ourselves lightly. Every little decision does not make or break the backbone of our lives. Things that seem huge one day can be relegated to the inconsequential by the next day.

Humor can offset and balance out intensity when we feel burdened and weighted down. We can consciously remember to lighten up, to not take ourselves so seriously, to not approach every little problem as a serious one—to spread our wings and lightly fly, rather than feel weighted down all day.

Today I will look at life in a lighter way, laugh more easily, and notice how much I can let go of a sense of burden.

February 17

Heartbreak is life educating us.
　　　　　　　　　　　・～ George Bernard Shaw

Heartbreaks come in many ways, some big and some small. Some might be accurately called disappointments, while others are full-blown sorrows. Each is real and palpable. What they all have in common is they cause us to see our lives more clearly, stripping away our illusions and pretenses. We learn a little bit more about ourselves, about the world around us, and about our needs.

Wherever there might be heartbreak in your life today, or in your child's life, know that it is a clarifying time. Difficult as it may be, the wiping clean of the emotional window frees you up for a more authentic life, a stronger match between your inner and outer life. There is a lot to be learned from this.

Wherever I see heartbreak I can also look for learning.

February 18

I have just three things to teach: simplicity, patience, compassion. These three are your greatest treasures.

– Lao Tzu

Living a full life as an adult and raising one or more children is a complicated and full endeavor. Whatever we can do to simplify our lives helps us focus on what is really important—which, to a great extent, is being our true selves and encouraging our children to do the same. The teen years are poignant for their formative qualities and for the experimenting and "trying on" that's all part of the process.

As we live with our children, teaching them, helping them, and at the same time living our own lives, patience and compassion will deepen our own self-acceptance and acceptance of who they are. Relax over the dyed hair, the baggy pants—dig a little deeper for what this young person is seeking, and keep it simple.

A quiet sense of compassion, hand in hand with a simple and straightforward approach, can make this day a treasure.

February 19

Swift gratitude is the sweetest.

                      ·~ Greek proverb

Lately I've been noticing what a treat it is to be around people who are appreciative. There's a positive sense to someone who is spontaneously and easily thankful for small and large things. This kind of appreciation is worth a lot in the midst of family life.

Pause and think about it: When was the last time you told your child thanks for walking the dog, thanks for doing the dishes, thanks for being kind to your brother, thanks for helping me bring in groceries, or thanks for being such a good student? There is a simple sweetness at the receiving end, knowing your gestures are appreciated.

Today I will contribute to family harmony by being grateful. The sweetness of gratitude is something I want my child to know.

February 20

Parenthood is just the world's most intensive course in love.

~ Polly Berrien Berends

The kind of love a parent has for a child encompasses so many feelings: everything from incredible tenderness to the heights of joy to the agony of heartache (and so many nuances in between). This love melts and reshapes us, and challenges us to stretch in multiple ways.

Along the way we learn a lot about who we are. We take shape like a mountain face carved by the elements, the wind forcing us to be strong in ourselves, the rain softening and deepening who we are, and the sun lighting up our lives. Over the course of our lives, our children will be the wind, rain, and sunshine that shape the mountain face of our ability to love.

Today I will honor how deep and profound the lessons of love are in my family life.

February 21

Accidents will occur in the best-regulated families.

.~ Charles Dickens

Accidents of all sorts happen in the course of family life and they are almost always inconvenient. If you're lucky, they are not tragic. The car accident a teen has that creates the irritation of a car in the shop for a week is something to be grateful for in lieu of a fatal accident.

Lost glasses that need to be replaced, a broken chair beyond repair, and the ripped jacket that needs mending—these are all part of the nature of the beast: humans make mistakes. As a parent, you don't need to blame, point fingers, or assign fault to yourself or to anyone else.

What accident do I need to put into a larger perspective today?

February 22

There are many times when we can't be there for our children. They need to be able to find adults who can help them and value them.

 ⌐ Patty Wetterling

An important thing we can do for our children is to encourage their healthy connections to other adults. There's a raft of possibilities: teachers, coaches, parents of their friends, relatives, neighbors. No one among us can meet all the needs our children have. And the more our kids get some of those needs met by other adults, the better it is for everybody.

When my daughter was experiencing the worst week of her sophomore year, it was her skating coach who helped soothe her more than I could. During that time, all those joyful years spent on the rink with an encouraging and loving adult came to a much-needed fruition. Her coach, a wise woman, knew her skaters needed emotional understanding and care in addition to practical knowledge of the sport. For my part, knowing I was delivering my daughter into loving arms eased my worry and concern.

I will encourage and express thanks to a significant adult in my child's life.

February 23

I have raised four teen girls and I'm convinced the key is for the mother to maintain her sense of self—because they will throw everything at her.

— Dr. Martha Hickner

Teens, by the very process of working to become independent, will try to attack, erode, and tear down their parents' sense of self. They will see us as stupid, worthy of disdain. They will be hypercritical. They will blame us. They will make our shortcomings glaringly apparent.

So it becomes paramount to hold onto a sense of self, whatever it takes. We never promised perfection and it's okay if we are not perfect parents or human beings. If we are to be at peace during these teen years we need to reach deep inside and feed our sense of self. We need to hold onto this self and nurture it, no matter what critical winds are blowing around us.

I will do one thing today that honors my positive sense of myself—this is an important part of what makes me a good parent.

February 24

According to Chesterton's cheerful view,
leisure was above all an opportunity to do
nothing. When he said "doing nothing" how-
ever, he was describing not emptiness but an
occasion for reflection and contemplation, a
chance to look inward rather than outward.
— Witold Rybczynski

We all want our children to be able to resist negative
peer pressure. Yet the ability to do so is based on
a strong inner sense of self and, in our fast-paced,
schedule-oriented, goal-focused culture, how and
when does one develop a strong sense of self?

It is good to encourage in our children (and
build into our own days) a few minutes of looking
inward rather than outward. There are many ways
to do this, but it requires slowing down and spending a few moments with oneself, alone. It can be
done through reading, fishing, playing a musical instrument, drawing, meditating, exercising, and many
other activities.

Today I will remember that a strong sense of self, for
me and for my child, requires a daily dose of quiet and
alone time.

February 25

Mama exhorted her children at every opportunity to "jump at de sun." We might not land on the sun, but at least we would get off the ground.

~ Zora Neale Hurston

If a child shows an inclination, an interest, a passion, then as parents we want to create a road with as many green lights as possible. Sometimes we unconsciously put up barriers, especially if we were limited in our own childhoods. Maybe we are too quick to point out what is impractical or expensive, or what seems too far-reaching or too edgy a dream.

Even when our children are interested in things we are not really comfortable or familiar with, we can be encouraging. If it's about developing a talent or interest, then it's all positive. Even if they decide to give up shooting for the moon (or the sun), at least we've helped them reach for it.

I will say or do one thing today that encourages my child to believe in and reach for a dream.

February 26

*Grant me the serenity to accept the things
I cannot change.*

~ The Serenity Prayer

This could be the parent mantra. How many times over the years have you bumped into the wall of what you cannot change? Why do you sometimes have to learn by banging your head first and most likely over and over again?

We cannot change core personalities. We cannot change life circumstances. We cannot change the choices our children make. Graceful acceptance and graceful letting go are worthy goals—hard to attain and hard to maintain but well worth the effort. And far more spiritually uplifting than head banging.

Today I will work on gracefully accepting one thing I cannot change about my child.

February 27

Everyone has a "risk muscle." You keep it in shape by trying new things. If you don't, it atrophies. Make a point of using it at least once a day.

-- Roger von Oech

So often the word "risk" is associated with un-healthy behaviors. Yet positive risks are important, for ourselves and for our kids. Part of our job as parents is to encourage them to take positive risks and to model the taking of positive risks ourselves.

It's a risk to try out for the school play, to write and then read a poem aloud, or to set a goal for higher grades. It's a positive risk to seek out a teacher when your teen needs help with a class. It's a risk for your child to try a new sport or push to new levels in a current activity. And as the parent, a positive risk might be going back to school or pursuing a new in-terest. Exercising the positive risk muscles makes life vibrant and interesting and keeps us growing.

I will stretch my risk muscle today and encourage my child to do the same.

February 28

Should you shield the canyons from the wind-storms, you would never see the beauty of their carvings.

— Dr. Elisabeth Kübler-Ross

Your child's heart has been broken for the first time. You watch your son struggle with homework day after day in a subject that is difficult for him. Your daughter, despite all her efforts, does not make the varsity team. Your child's feelings are hurt by her friends.

You cannot shield your child from these things, these normal ups and downs. They are the wind-storms of adolescence, and they do indeed shape a person. How your child responds, copes, and manages is all part of what shapes the emotional carving that is distinctive, individual, and in its own way beautiful.

Today I will try not to shield my child too much. Instead, I will respect the sensitive shape that is emerging.

March 1

*It is only with the heart that one can see
rightly; what is essential is invisible to the eye.*
- Antoine de Saint-Exupéry

Often parenting requires a sixth sense, a seeing with
the heart rather than cold hard facts. Since we don't
always have full access to information, we often need
to engage in a sort of inner listening to our child.
Does she seem particularly subdued? Do you sense
a lack of honesty on the part of your teen? Are you
concerned about new friends who don't seem to be
positive influences?

It is usually constructive to express these concerns, but most importantly, you must honor what
your heart is feeling and noticing in your teen's behavior, demeanor, or mood. If your teen seems lonely
and more in need of affection than usual, where else
would you get this information?

*What is tugging at my heart today? I will pay atten-
tion to it.*

March 2

*It is surprising how much memory is built
around things unnoticed at the time.*

— Barbara Kingsolver

Memory is experienced subjectively. It is so hard to know what our children will remember—often it is the subtle and quiet gestures and moments. All the small ways we let our teenagers know they are safe and respected filter into their memory pool somewhere and somehow. The times and ways we allow our children to make their own decisions also hold a special place in their memories.

Perhaps more than anything, it is the small, daily ways we care for our children that build the strongest memory base.

*Today I will trust that the base of love I give my teen-
ager will remain in her memory for the rest of her life.*

March 3

*Have regular conversations with your sons
and daughters about sex and sexuality.
Don't keep quiet and let TV and movies
become the only teachers your kids have.*

·~ Dr. David Walsh

TV shows and movies can actually provide great opportunities for parents to talk about what they agree
or don't agree with. A TV show that is watched together can open doors for discussion about values
around our bodies and how we and our teens take
care of them.

Never easy, usually awkward, the more you can
be casual, humorous, or just plain honest, the better
these conversations will go. And as much as your
child may not respond with interest, all our children need to hear that if they have questions, they
can come to you. Keep saying it.

*I will do what I can do to open the doors for any tough
conversations about sexuality.*

March 4

If a child shows great commitment to something, it is easier to transfer to other things later.

.- Doris Bodmer

My daughter was an avid figure skater for about ten years and then left the sport so she could focus more on academics, other sports, and activities. A lot of time, effort, financial support, and energy went into those years of skating, and it would have been easy to wonder if it was worth it.

For many reasons the answer is yes, but perhaps above all because she practiced dedication and discipline. She learned teamwork and the value of having another trusted adult (her coach) who cared about her. The practice of being committed and the rewards of that daily dedication are seeds that will bear fruit in many areas of her life. It feels good to know that we encouraged and made this kind of commitment possible.

Today I will look at the areas of commitment in my teen's life. I will verbally honor them and do one concrete thing to make them more possible.

March 5

A faithful friend is the medicine of life.
— The Apocrypha

Think of the things medicine does for us. Sometimes it eases pain. Other times it helps us heal. It clears up infections and eases many small aches and pains.

It is our friends, our true friends, who help us to heal when we are broken, who ease the pain of our losses. Laughter has been linked to medicine, and it is the friends who laugh with us who also help us heal and hang in for the long haul. Most of us would say we want our children to know how to be a friend and how to have friends. We do this by modeling our own friendships.

The joy and comfort of the friendships in my life are gifts to myself and to my child.

March 6

*I think I could turn and live with ani-
mals . . . / They do not sweat and whine
about their condition . . . / Not one is
dissatisfied. . . .*

·~ Walt Whitman

Adolescence is often a time of anxiousness and long-
ing. Raising adolescents can be an on-the-edge, nerve-
wracking experience. And although an occasional
healthy dose of whining helps to get it out of the sys-
tem, the point is always to move toward contentment.

Instead of feeling dissatisfied with aspects of
our own lives or dissatisfied with some part of our
teenager's life, we can notice what we have and what
is going well. With a simple twist of consciousness,
we can move from whining to appreciating.

*Like the birds outside my window, I can find something
to sing about today. In this way, I model the simple values of contentment and appreciation for today's gifts.*

March 7

The nourisher must learn to be nourished.
·- T. D. Jakes

As parents, we are the nourishers. From Day One, we provide our children with food, shelter, and a sense of safety. We also provide life lessons, miles of driving, emotional support, guidance, and a host of other things. As the primary nourishers in our teen children's lives, we need to remember to nourish ourselves.

Just as a teacher relearns by occasionally becoming a student again, so we learn by allowing ourselves to be nourished. To seek out and receive emotional support can be a lifeline, a lesson in reciprocity. It teaches us the beauty of receiving and the importance of such a gift for ourselves and our children. It also deepens the reservoir we are able to draw upon.

Today I will find a way to nourish myself.

March 8

*Once you've articulated your family bound-
aries, expect your children to honor them.
Don't suspect them of misbehavior without
a reason.*

> ·– *What Kids Need to Succeed:*
> *Proven, Practical Ways*
> *to Raise Good Kids*

Family boundaries around behavior, curfew, and
school performance are important to clarify (and
from time to time renegotiate) with your child.
They are made clear by talking about them or even
posting them.

It's much better to be positive in your expectations than suspicious. If you expect teens to follow
the rules, most will (at least pretty closely). If you
don't expect teens to follow the rules and have no
concrete reason for distrusting them, it's time to
back off and work on your own thinking. Children
know when they are being unfairly accused and it
usually doesn't bring out the best in them. Expecting
the best is far better than inviting the worst.

*Today I will work on expecting the best from my chil-
dren. If the worst arrives on my doorstep, I can deal with
it knowing I didn't invite it.*

March 9

Innocence is the knowledge that love is deeper than surface events.

.- Deepak Chopra

So often we get caught up in the events of the day—an argument over something our teen wants to buy, a disagreement about chores, the dizzying demands of a particular time.

Whatever the surface tension in our lives today, we can remember the currents of love running beneath. Whitecaps on the water are part of the storms of parent-child dynamics. Instead of getting hung up on surface struggles, we can remember the deep springs of love swirling below. As difficult as windy days can be, the deeper love is always there, nourishing us and our children.

Today I will remember the depth of my love for my child, and know, deep in my heart, that it will teach me how to sail through even the windiest and stormiest of times.

March 10

All of your "God" words / will not teach your children as much / as will your nurture, / and your love, / and your cherishing.

.- William Martin

I remember, when I was a child, how my visions of God seemed to go hand-in-hand with my visions of my parents and other authority figures. Adolescent years began the process of wrestling with my own ideas and images of spirituality. As part of my internal discussion I was ever on the alert for mixed messages about what my parents preached and how they lived it.

Whatever our own religious and spiritual beliefs are, the way we live them is more powerful than what we have to say about them. Talking and discussion have their place, but how we treat and love our children sends the strongest message of all.

Today I will express my spiritual values through actions or gestures.

March 11

Life isn't a matter of milestones, but of moments.

~ Rose Kennedy

A day comes along when you and your children linger at the table after dinner, laughing and chatting, and you realize, we all like each other. We all enjoy each other's company. Today.

Last week there was a yelling match in the family, but you salvaged the day by taking a walk in the evening with a friend. The sunset reflected on the lake was spectacular that night, and hope reentered you. Your son, who often barely speaks to you, gives you a hug when you talk about a disappointment at work. His hug feels completely healing to you. These are the moments to be savored, the moments that make life meaningful.

Today I will notice and be grateful for the moments that really count in my life.

March 12

I have seen the sea when it is stormy and
wild; when it is quiet and serene; when it
is dark and moody. And in all its moods,
I see myself.

— Martin Buxbaum

So often as a culture we narrow the range for acceptable moods and feelings. Sometimes parents impose narrow emotional expectations on their teenage children, forgetting that human beings are capable of expressing many shades of feelings. If we have a favorite body of water, it's worth noticing the many nuances to its moods, how each day can be slightly different, and how the mood of the water changes throughout the day.

Because teen years are moody years, we need to understand the depth and variety of moods that are possible in the human experience. Because moods are strangely contagious, we also need to pay attention to and monitor our own. It's healthy to accept a full palate of moods without imposing one's mood on another.

I do not have to be at the mercy of my teen's moods,
and I can accept that they are as varied as the forces of
wind and weather at work in the world around us.

March 13

*Think of all the beauty still left around you
and be happy.*

— Anne Frank

Appreciation of beauty in the world around us is connected to a sense of hope. If Anne Frank, living in dire circumstances, could find hope and happiness just in thinking of beauty, then surely our own sensory experience of beauty can uplift us no matter what kind of day we are having.

Each day provides natural beauty in a sunrise and sunset, in trees, flowers, blossoms, and landscapes of all seasons and moods. Often at our fingertips are experiences in the visual arts, in music or dance, or in the song of the birds. All we have to do is notice and allow it into our hearts. What a wonderful and helpful lesson to share with our children.

*Today I will let an experience of beauty into my heart
and share my happiness with my children.*

March 14

*What marks the artist is his power to shape
the material of pain we all have.*

·- Lionel Trilling

A painting, a sculpture, or a piece of music can stir a sense of recognition. As we listen or observe, feelings of sadness or hope may shine through, even if it's hard to articulate exactly why. When we listen to the blues we feel the sadness, but at the same time we want to tap our feet.

Artistry of all sorts comforts our souls because it shapes the pain that is part of the universal human experience. The shape of a song or painting often gives us a sense of wholeness. If an artist can make a creation out of pain, then we can all creatively work with and heal our pain.

Today I will immerse myself in the healing quality of art, be it visual, musical, or otherwise.

March 15

*Children are extraordinarily precious
members of a society; they are exquisitely
alert, sensitive, and conscious of their
surroundings.*

– Barbara Coloroso

One of the great things about hanging around with
kids is how they keep opening our hearts and minds.
They are fresher in how they perceive the world; their
youthful energy sharpens what they notice around
them. They are more open to change, to what is new.

If a teenager questions one of your long-held
beliefs, consider it a good and worthwhile question,
one worth learning from. If a teenager introduces
you to a new and thought-provoking piece of music,
thank her or him. If a child points out what your
family is lacking, come up with a plan to implement
a change. Such awarenesses are all good.

*I am thankful today for the fresh perspective my child
brings into my life.*

March 16

He that would be a leader must be a bridge.
— Welsh proverb

The most successful leaders in the world are the ones who can connect with people, who can motivate and inspire them. One cannot lead effectively from a remote distance. As parents we want to lead our children, as well as inspire and motivate them.

But like a bridge reaching across a ravine, we need to reach out, walk toward, and pave the way between ourselves and our teens. Some concrete ways to do this are: meet their friends; invite their friends over; take them to places that interest them; help make an extracurricular activity possible. Keep building a bridge from your world to theirs and then gently invite them to follow your lead.

I will do one thing today to bridge my world and my teen's.

March 17

Faith is the bird that feels the light and sings when the dawn is still dark.

— Rabindranath Tagore

When you are going through a dark time as a parent—whether the worry is small or large—the nights can seem long. Worry loves the dark and quiet of night time. Worry robs us of much needed rest.

There's only so much we can do to take care of any problem; the rest is beyond our control. We need to turn over that uncontrollable part to forces greater than ourselves. Whatever we put our faith in—and as a diverse people there are many forms and visions of faith—this is the time to draw on that well of strength. We need to believe that whatever we are worried about will resolve, heal, and get worked out. We must trust that things will get better.

Today I will rely on whatever form of faith I have and believe that a certain area of my life or my teen's life will get better.

March 18

*I keep the telephone of my mind open to
peace, harmony, health, love, and abundance. Then whenever doubt, anxiety, or
fear try to call me, they keep getting a busy
signal and soon they'll forget my number.*

·- Edith Armstrong

We have the double-edged challenge as parents to
live our own lives in a positive and hopeful manner
and to teach our children how to live such lives at
the same time. There's a double consciousness involved here, but it really does begin with ourselves.
To a certain extent we can choose our outlook and
attitude.

I love the idea of attitude being a telephone
line, a circuit running between ourselves and the
world around us. If we fill this link with feelings of
love, peace, harmony, health, and abundance, then
it is much harder for negative emotions to squeak
through. When they do, we can dial up and connect, consciously, with the positive circuit.

*Today I will reach out to whomever and whatever helps
me be a positive person, for myself and for my child.*

March 19

*One of the secrets of life is to make stepping
stones out of stumbling blocks.*

— Dr. Jack Penn

I recently heard a teacher talk about a student who
didn't make it into the school play but came to her
and said, "I want to be involved. I will do anything
you need me to do." This student became an invaluable part of the production team and won a special
award for her work at year's end. The student herself raved about how much she learned about all the
other parts of play production besides acting.

Here is a young woman who took what must
have initially felt like a stumbling block and turned
it into a stepping-stone to another way of learning
and involvement in what she loves. This is the kind
of optimism and resiliency we ideally want to encourage in our children. Perhaps part of our job is
to help our children see pathways around a block.
Most likely this student had a parent who encouraged her all the way.

*Today I will show my teen one way to turn an obstacle
into an opportunity.*

March 20

I don't ask for the meaning of the song of a bird or the rising of the sun on a misty morning. There they are, and they are beautiful.
                                        — Pete Hamill

There are some things in life we can count on, without having to question the why, how, or what of them. Nature's gifts are this: there for us to enjoy, there to lift our spirits. If we can remember this when we are struggling with issues, as a human being or as a parent, we can reach out for this comfort, which is always nearby.

If your teenager sees that it helps you to process the loss of your parent by taking long walks by a nearby river, he or she learns the comforts of nature, which exist separately from the complications of relationships. If your teen sees how the beauty of the sunset makes you happy, you are modeling the notion that beauty is out there, waiting for us to enjoy it.

Today I will enjoy the music in birdsong or the beautiful sky at dusk, and share this simple joy with my teenager. Even if he doesn't get it now, he will later.

March 21

A baby is born with a need to be loved—and never outgrows it.

.- Frank A. Clark

Those sweet adorable babies sometimes grow into teenagers who are moody and prickly or easily upset. Their need to be loved can be well-disguised at times, but it's always there.

They may blow off your compliments or shy away from a gesture of affection, but think of a time when you pushed away something you also really wanted. As a parent, it can be hard to give when you are unsure of how you'll be received. But your child needs ample amounts of both your approval and affection. You can always try a lighter touch or a new approach, but above all, keep letting your child know you love him or her.

I will look beyond the prickly outer edge of my child and remember, through what I say or do, the love I always have for my child.

March 22

Adolescents sometimes say, "My friends listen to me, but my parents only hear me talk." Often they are right. Familiarity breeds inattention.

‑ You and Your Adolescent:
A Parent's Guide for Ages 10–20

Friends whose parent-child relationships I admire greet their children in a friendly way, ask a specific question about their day, and really *listen* to their teens when they walk through the door. When kids share something with you about their day, they'll know you are listening by your response, your questions, and your sense of caring about what they're saying. If you respond absentmindedly when your thoughts are elsewhere, they'll probably quit talking.

Some children are less talkative than others. They may go through phases when they don't want to share much. Sometimes you can't seem to get *anything* out of them. But when teens do talk, you can make listening a priority. Clear the worry about tomorrow's schedule from your brain. Know that listening is the most important thing you can do right now.

For the few moments my teenager feels like sharing, nothing is more important than my simply listening.

March 23

Perhaps the hardest part about being the parent of a teenager is that though parents must let go, they must also be there to provide love and support.

— Dr. Anthony E. Wolf

Letting go and being there are opposite ends of the same seesaw. One without the other might be easier, but the two provide the needed balance in parenting. The key is to determine which end of the seesaw needs to be up at any given moment.

You let your teen make a decision regarding something and it doesn't go well. Part of you wants to say, "I told you so," but instead you keep it to yourself and support her. What your teen has done, besides making a less-than-perfect choice, is taking a step toward independence. This is all part of the learning teens must go through, and when they make those mistakes we need to be there and help them. Who among us hasn't made mistakes? And we have all needed to feel loved in spite of them.

I will pay attention today to the seesaw balance between myself and my teen. Is today a day I need to let go or a day I need to be there?

March 24

I lived in the rhythms of other people's lives.
.– Adrienne Rich

The demands of parenting are such that we sometimes find our days revolving around our children's
needs and schedules. To a certain extent, this is part
of the job requirement.

But it's also important to take time to remember and rediscover our own rhythms. Sometimes
a trip away from home does this. Or taking a class
and claiming one night a week as your time. Maybe
it's taking a day once in a while to treat yourself in
your favorite ways. As hard as it is to believe, one
day our children will take their rhythms and leave.
The transition will be easier if we have kept some
sense of our own rhythms.

*This week I will do one concrete thing to remember my
rhythms, especially if I'm feeling buried by other people's.*

March 25

*Take a chance! All life is a chance. The man
who goes furthest is generally the one who is
willing to do and dare.*

·– Dale Carnegie

Teens need encouragement to pursue their dreams
and goals. It's never easy at any age to go out on a
limb, to take a chance. It truly does require courage and that magical quality of get-up-and-go or
chutzpah.

Say your teen wants to audition for a school
play for the first time or try out for varsity track. Or
maybe your teen wants to join the debate team, write
and publish a story, or perform in a band. These and
all their other first steps out in the world to explore
their talents and interests are good steps, learning
steps, stretching steps. As adults we can clear the
way, cheer from the sidelines, and, once in a while,
model the same adventurousness in our own lives.

*I will notice today where my teen might need encour-
agement to step out a little, or where I might need to
just appreciate a step that's already been taken.*

March 26

Envy is the art of counting the other fellow's blessings instead of your own.

.-- Harold Coffin

Most of us tend to run into parent-envy once in a while. It works along the lines of: why aren't my daughter's grades as good as her daughter's? Or, why is my son overweight no matter how I try to help him, but my friend's kids seem to have no concerns in this department? How come my neighbor's family looks so perfect, especially on the days when nothing seems to be right at our house?

There's such truth to the adage "you can't judge a book by its cover." Nothing is as perfect and seamless as it can sometimes look. And the act of comparing ourselves to others, or our children to others, is always a fruitless proposition. It's an easy way to completely miss seeing what is right and good within our own lives.

Today I will consciously count my blessings, as a human being and as a parent.

March 27

A discussion is a process by which we try to come to the best possible solution of any problem that confronts us for the benefit of all concerned.

~ Dr. Rudolf Dreikurs

Problems are part of family life. And so we could ignore them, or yell about them, or have a discussion to work toward resolving them. If someone in the family isn't doing her or his chores or if someone is being especially moody and making life hard for everyone else, it can be helpful to choose to talk at a time that is not in the heat of the moment.

As parents this is something we can institute any time we feel the need. We can also give our children permission to request such a meeting of the minds. It's vital to stress that everyone gets a chance to be heard—and to see that it actually happens.

If there's a problem, we can work toward solving it by putting our heads together and talking.

March 28

If we don't change, we don't grow. If we don't grow, we aren't really living.

— Gail Sheehy

Although the change and growth of our children can elicit mixed feelings in most of us, it is part of the journey. The teen who is immersed in her first love is at the beginning of what we know to be a long and complicated journey. We're happy for her, worried for her. The teen who is going through his first heartbreak breaks our hearts as well, as we watch and try to help.

Every new stage in our children's lives is both exciting and sad as we say goodbye to a former stage that we will most likely miss. And yet, it wouldn't feel right if our teens didn't change and grow. It requires openness and optimism to embrace these changes and mixed emotions.

Today I will see the change in my child as an opportunity to optimistically embrace growth.

March 29

*The healthy, the strong individual, is the one
who asks for help when he needs it. Whether
he's got an abscess on his knee or his soul.*

— Rona Barrett

Nothing separates us more as parents than competitiveness over our children, and nothing connects us quite like our vulnerabilities about our children. When you are struggling with your kids, it always helps to find others who have had similar struggles. It also helps to have a compassionate friend who understands even if he or she hasn't been through it.

Sometimes we keep everything to ourselves for too long—keeping up the pretense, or perhaps the wish, that everything is just fine. Yet when we break through and open up, there is immense relief. Support, comfort, and even some solutions can come to us if we are healthy and courageous enough to be vulnerable.

When I need help or guidance I will see it as a sign of my health to ask for it.

March 30

Giving is the secret of a healthy life. Not necessarily money but whatever a person has of encouragement, sympathy and understanding.

⁓ John D. Rockefeller Jr.

It is strange and remarkable how much giving does for the giver. Most of us feel more useful and more worthwhile when we give of ourselves—of our talents, our time, our care. When I stop my merry-go-round schedule long enough to chat with my 90-year-old neighbor, it's a good day. I hope when I am her age that there are neighbors who visit me.

I want my children to see that it's important to take time to help where help is needed, however they can. Giving may take on a wide variety of forms, but so long as it's done in a sincere and empathetic spirit, it will always be healing for everyone involved.

Today I will give time or encouragement to someone around me who is in need, and I will encourage this impulse in my child.

March 31

Cleaning your house while your kids are still growing is like shoveling the walk before it stops snowing.

— Phyllis Diller

There are many things a person gives up when becoming a parent, and having a tidy house all or most of the time is usually one of them. I know several empty-nesters who sheepishly admit how much they enjoy being able to keep a house in order, how amazing it is that things get put away and stay away.

I also know more than one active parent who talks of how the dirty socks and athletic equipment, the stacks of laundry and paperwork pile up. More people, more clutter. We may have it all in order one day or one week, but with children it takes very little time for the wild, untamed mess to return. Remember, wildness is very alive.

My children can be trained to shovel the walk, but will need to be reminded. In the meantime, I can enjoy the bounty of snowfall and loving children around me.

April 1

I have seen what a laugh can do. It can trans-
form almost unbearable tears into something
bearable, even hopeful.

— Bob Hope

Laughter with friends, a sense of humor that is
shared or private, can go a long way to healing us,
saving us, and sustaining us. For example, there is
something rather humorous in finding ourselves
saying and doing things that remind us of our own
parents. And, even in the midst of our deepest worries or our worst tragedies, there can be something
that strikes us as funny, especially if we allow ourselves a wide-angle, full-scope vision.

As long as we can laugh, we know we will survive. That is the hopeful part of laughter—it brings
in enough light to outshine whatever darkness is
currently around us.

Today I will look for the humorous light in my darkness
and laugh to myself or with a good friend.

April 2

The function of the wing is to take what is heavy and raise it up into the region above, where the gods dwell.

— Plato

All of us have heavy days as parents. Days when the task of being a parent feels like a very heavy burden. Days when a conflict with a teen feels like a boulder across our shoulders. Days when a worry or concern for a child feels much heavier than gravity.

I like the idea of wings taking what is heavy in our hearts up toward the gods. No matter what our spiritual beliefs are, the idea of lifting our burdens into the open arms of a benevolent force can bring comfort. Sometimes, when it's too much for us to bear alone, we need to turn our troubles over to a greater power, however we perceive that power.

In my own way, I can ask for spiritual help with my problems as a parent.

April 3

What is it to be the parent of a teenager?
It is to do what you think best—when really
you have no idea what is best.

— Dr. Anthony E. Wolf

One has to have a sense of humor to appreciate the cosmic joke of this conundrum. And if only it were a more humorous experience! Unfortunately, it is often agonizing and mind-bending to try to figure out the right thing when no solution comes with any guarantees or even any best guesses of outcomes.

It is hard, and perhaps impossible, to ever truly know what is best for our children. We need to do what we think is best, and most of us arrive at that best guess with a little help. Here is where any available support sources are needed—a good friend, a support group, your partner or spouse, family friends, books, professionals. Whatever helps us feel and think more clearly—it is easier to know what is right in any given situation after a good night's sleep, a long walk, or some meditation or prayer time.

If I am struggling to find the best response to my teen,
I will seek resources for help and make time to carefully
consider the issue today.

April 4

Consider now a particular behavior that concerns you. / Meditate carefully and see through / to the heart of your child. / What does it tell you?

— William Martin

Most of us have an immediate reaction when trouble hits our kids. Who doesn't prefer a day of smooth sailing? Yet trouble can bring us an opportunity to look more closely at our child. What is he struggling with, and what issues swirl around his academic or social life? What does her behavior tell you about her world?

Behavior that concerns us should give us pause. In slowing down, looking deeper into the matter at hand, we may move closer to knowing our child. It's a time to listen and reflect, far beyond our initial kneejerk reactions.

I can look at behavior that concerns me as a path toward (or at least a road sign to) what is stirring in the heart of my child.

April 5

*If you don't take personal offense at your
teen's behavior, you'll be better able to deal
with the issue that's important.*

— Dr. Susan Panzarine

Not taking your child's behavior personally is much
easier said than done. When a teen is struggling
with typical adolescent issues, the easiest target in
the world is the parent who's there. A discussion
about a homework project or chore they need to do
can easily explode into a tirade about what a mean
parent you are.

Steel yourself, count to ten, take three deep
breaths. Do whatever it takes to not get hooked
into defending yourself. Keep the focus where it belongs by staying strong and clear.

*Today I will work at not letting my teenager's emotional
ups and downs cloud my sense of what he or she needs.*

April 6

*Adolescence is that period in kids' lives when
their parents become more difficult.*

.- Ryan O'Neal

It is never easy on the ego to be thought of as less
than intelligent or cool. And yet as parents we are
destined to be seen in this way. We may have been
intelligent all of our lives, we may be seen as cool
among our friends and colleagues, and our children
probably admired us a great deal at one time.

But in the teen years it's a different story. Suddenly the son who always wanted you to volunteer
in grade school now wants you nowhere near him
in high school. The daughter who used to ask for
your advice now does the opposite of what you suggest. One has to work hard to maintain a sense of
self. It helps to know you are not alone, and it also
helps to have friends to remind you that you are
just as cool and intelligent as ever, no matter what
your teen says.

*The rocks in the road between me and my teen are part of
the path that adolescents forge on the way to adulthood.*

April 7

The world's great age begins anew, / The golden years return, / The earth doth like a snake renew / Her winter weeds outworn.

·- Percy Bysshe Shelley

The idea of rebirth is a theme that runs through the ethos of almost all cultural groups. And it is almost always celebrated in the spring, that time when nature is also regenerating and giving birth to new plants, trees, flowers. This is a good time as parents to touch base with our own rituals, and to expose and teach our children about other cultures' ways of expressing this theme.

What Native American myths, Christianity's Easter, Judaism's Rosh Hashanah, the spring equinox, and others have in common is the idea that the old dies to make way for the new. It's about rebirth and transformation. These truths are ancient, universal, and above all hopeful. It's a good opportunity to point out connective threads between cultures, to share this knowledge with our children.

I will do one thing in this season to celebrate the concept of rebirth and transformation and share it with my child.

April 8

Life is denied by lack of attention, whether it be to cleaning windows or trying to write a masterpiece.

~ Nadia Boulanger

More than anything, our children need and deserve attention from us. It's a simple gift and one that can easily be overlooked when life fills up with other commitments. Two things matter here: one is time, although it doesn't necessarily require a lot of time, and two is the ability to focus completely and directly on our children.

Eye contact is important. Simple conversation is important. Checking in with them about how a test or event went for them is a way of touching base. Going with them to do an errand is a great way to be together, and also provides an opportunity for talking. Even when they don't offer much in return, it's important to give them, daily, the simple gift of attention.

Today I will take at least a few minutes to touch base and pay attention to each of my children.

April 9

You cannot mother well when you feel overwhelmed.

~ Esther Davis-Thompson

From time to time all of us feel overwhelmed. Perhaps you are behind on housework, a big project at work, or the papers piled up on the dining room table. Perhaps you have just lost a dearly beloved family member, or are stretched thin taking care of an elderly parent. Perhaps you were just laid off from your job and can't imagine how you will keep paying bills.

Whatever the particulars of feeling overwhelmed, we need to realize that it's not a strong place to parent from. Being overwhelmed weakens our sense of strength and clouds our judgment. So, first things first. We need to sort through what is overwhelming us and get help or take action. We owe it to who we are as parents to take care of ourselves.

Today I will take a concrete step to understanding and dealing with why I am overwhelmed.

April 10

Forgiveness is like faith. You have to keep reviving it.

— Mason Cooley

There are days as a parent when you or your teen could use forgiveness. If a child has been particularly hard on you, this can feel like the last thing you are able to do. If you have made mistakes—lost your temper, or failed to do something you promised to do—it can be tough to forgive yourself.

Sometimes one must start with the baby step of asking for the willingness to forgive, of asking for some melting of the cold hard rock of anger. That rock of anger can be hard to let go of and most likely needs to be talked or worked through in some way. Letting go and being able to forgive is a process that requires, at the outset, a small sliver of willingness.

Whom and what do I need to forgive today? If I'm not there yet, I can begin to think about being will-ing to be there.

April 11

Children are likely to live up to what you believe of them.

— Lady Bird Johnson

There is no underestimating the power of this: What we believe of our children has a huge impact on them. If we expect them to do well as students, to be involved, to care about others, to be a good friend, then we help pave the way for those actions. Of course they ultimately do these things themselves. Yet parents who see their children in a positive light and admire their kindnesses and abilities are ones who foster growth in all these areas.

If we find ourselves expecting the worst, perhaps we need to look at our own fears. Parenting from a position of love rather than fear is far more healing and hopeful.

Today I will parent with love, not fear.

April 12

*Every parent is at some time the father of the
unreturned prodigal, with nothing to do but
keep his house open to hope.*

— John Ciardi

Your son falls head over heels in love and is gone all
the time—way overboard in your estimation. Your
daughter locks herself in her room these days and listens to harsh music. In worst-case scenarios, a child
runs away, or is overtly drinking and taking drugs.
If an intervention seems necessary, there are people
who can help. But even interventions don't bring a
child back to life at home, at least not right away.

When you have done all you can do, all that is
left is to be there and to hang onto a thread of hope
that your child will return, intact. Hope is an essential quality here—hope for the best outcome for
your child.

*Today I will light a candle of hope for some part of my
child I am concerned about.*

April 13

You may give them your love but not your thoughts. / For they have their own thoughts.
— Kahlil Gibran

From time to time most of us find ourselves in a position we never thought we'd be in—acting and sounding like our own parents. Who among us hasn't tried to change our child's thoughts about clothing, music, hair, or appearance? Or career choice, class choices, and friends?

Teens have their own thoughts and opinions, and a right to them. So, rather than giving them "a piece of your mind," give them your love. That is what is truly ours to give.

Rather than give my opinion today, I will focus on giving my love.

April 14

What is it to be the parent of a teenager? . . .
It is to give love to a child who does not seem
to want it.

— Dr. Anthony E. Wolf

The key word here is "seem." Our teens do not *seem*
to want our affection, doing very little in response
to our efforts and giving back very little at this point
in time.

For this reason, parenting is a deeply spiritual
river. We learn to give without measuring what we
get in return (ideally). This is the thankless aspect
of being a parent, but it is one we share with many
others. And there is a deep satisfaction in guiding
and nourishing another human being. Even though
our teens seem like they don't want our love, they
really do. They need to know that your love is a
candle burning deep into the night, relit anew each
morning.

Today I will love my child, no matter how that love is
received.

April 15

Money—the one thing that keeps us in touch with our children.

— Gyles Brandreth

Several parents I know have a running joke about how money flies out of their pockets when their teenagers are around. There seems to be no end to the requests for money for clothes, sports equipment, field trips, movies, lunches, and a host of other things.

It's important to be clear with teens about what you will pay for, what you won't, and what you expect in return. Beyond that, remember that in this day and age, the vast majority of teenagers will ask for money at one time or another. And it is a tangible connecting point, one I find myself strangely appreciating when there seem to be so few other ways my children still need me.

If my wallet is lighter because of my teenager, I can remember to set my limits and appreciate how money keeps us connected.

April 16

Alcohol has been and continues to be the substance that does the most damage to the most kids. . . . Alcohol drinking should be taken seriously, because it is so prevalent.
— Dr. David Walsh

As much as we dislike the reality, our children are faced with conversations, choices, and the availability of alcohol on a regular basis. Our job is not to brush it away or ignore its presence, but to set clear expectations and to talk about it. Children need the clarity of our clear expectations to balance out peer pressure and their own doubts and confusions.

Part of our job is to be open to conversation, to gently ask the right questions at the right time. Articles, books, or the information that a neighborhood boy was involved in a drunk driving accident are all food for conversation. Part of knowing our kids' world is knowing how much they have to deal with substance use and abuse.

Today I will not ignore this tough issue, nor will I blame my child for its existence.

April 17

Anything will give up its secrets if you love it enough.

– George Washington Carver

Most children keep a small or large part of their lives to themselves. As always, there is a fine line between respecting their rights to privacy and sensing when they have something they might need to talk about.

Although asking questions of them is fair, asking more than once can easily be construed as hounding. Rather, be a loving presence—affectionate, friendly, open. They may want to talk at the most surprising moments. If we're open and ready, we can meet them halfway.

Today I will remember that love is the opener to any conversation between me and my child.

April 18

People become really quite remarkable when they start thinking that they can do things. When they believe in themselves they have the first secret of success.

― Norman Vincent Peale

Belief in their abilities is the key to our kids' positive development. And although the hills and valleys of adolescence generate a phase or two of self-doubt in almost every child, we always want to help them find a way back to feeling good about who they are.

Easier said than done? An important step is believing in them ourselves. This means taking time to focus on their strong points, their talents, and their skills, and expressing what we notice. It also means helping them find ways to explore and expand their skills. Skill-building is an important facet of self-esteem. We want to do everything we can to help them believe in themselves—this is an important cornerstone to their success in whatever they choose to do.

Today I will take time to let my child know how capable he or she is.

April 19

Fear is the main source of superstition, and one of the main sources of cruelty. To conquer fear is the beginning of wisdom.

— Bertrand Russell

It's easy to feel fear for our children. We know the hazards of the world. We fear for their safety, for the risks that will confront them, and for the risk factors they carry within them. We send them off to camp and fret about whether they will eat and sleep and feel comfortable away from home. We send them off to school and worry about their exposure to alcohol and other drugs. And there's a barrel full of other potential things to fear.

But what fear really does is tighten our hearts and narrow our vision. Fear projects darkly into the future. When you feel fear clutching at your heart and tainting your thinking, it is worth every ounce of effort on your part to transform that fear into faith. You can learn to trust that you will know what to do for your child in this moment and in the next as well. You can trust that your child is on the road she needs to be on, even if it is a bumpy one.

Today I will write down one fear I have and burn it, letting go of it. I will write an affirmation to replace it.

April 20

*None but those who are happy in themselves
can make others so.*

— William Hazlitt

To a certain extent, happiness is fleeting. But most
of us know people who are usually happy and content, and most of us know those who are usually
unhappy and discontented. If we as parents want
a mostly happy family life and want to raise happy
children, we will need to seek out this quality in
ourselves.

What makes you happy or peaceful? What passions do you have? And how and when do you carve
out time for them? What we model is what our children learn, and an inner contentedness and happiness is contagious.

*I will look today at what makes me happy as a first step
to helping others around me be happy.*

April 21

You have all the courage you need; the more
you use, the more you will have.

- Growing Up Again:
Parenting Ourselves,
Parenting Our Children

When I think of courage in parenting I think of a
friend of mine. After many months of struggling
with her son's drug abuse—trying one program
and then another, living with the ongoing ups and
downs of addiction—she decided on a dramatic
route. She knew of a program that would work for
her son if any would. But it required sending the
boy away, suddenly and with no warning, into the
hands of able and caring adults well-versed in adolescent addiction.

The morning she sent her son away required
huge courage. So did all the days leading up to it
and away from it into a new future. Challenging
kids require deeper pockets of courage from their
parents. But from time to time we all need to dig
deep to do what we believe and know our child
needs, even if it's a hard or bumpy road.

If my child is in danger, I will have the courage to take
action today.

April 22

*Most of us can remember a special teacher
who refused to give up on us . . . or called
attention to a gift no one saw before. . . .
Let those teachers know you appreciate
those efforts!*

— Kathleen Kimball-Baker

The phrase "it takes a whole village to raise a child"
is frequently used because of the solid wisdom embedded in it. In raising a healthy, beloved human
being, teachers are an invaluable resource. They see
our children in a whole different context from the
one in which we parents see them.

As parents, we can let those special teachers
know we appreciate what they do for our children.
We can keep the lines of communication open between us and them. We can honor teachers for
being an invaluable and extremely helpful part of
this team effort.

*I will make the effort to thank a special teacher in my
teen's life, strengthening the web of care for my child.*

April 23

Lingering / rivers and mountains brighten
Spring winds / flowers and grass give out
scent.

— Tu Fu

There is much about nature that is healing, both for us and for our children. We have a love of water in our family, and the day my daughter had an important audition she and I first stopped at a nearby lake. Together we soaked up the sight and sound of water and the energy of the wind blowing across our faces.

I had been wracking my brain for what to do or say to encourage her for what was ahead. In the end, the world of water and wind did it for me. I simply took her there and all the memories of special times by water took over. She felt confident walking into her audition.

When I need to, I can use the comfort or energy of the natural world to inspire me and my child.

April 24

*When you stay connected you, too, enjoy these
[creative and fun] aspects of your teenager;
and in doing so, you regularly replenish your
parenting batteries.*

— Dr. Michael Riera

One early spring evening my daughter called me
from her cell phone and said, "Mom, it's beautiful
outside. Let's skate to a restaurant for dinner." I had
planned a more economical dinner at home, but
something wise took over in me. I decided my dinner plan would be just as good the following night,
and I said sure.

She, her good friend, my son, and I snapped on
our skates. We moved through the lovely spring air
together. They sang part of the time. We all reveled
in what a beautiful evening it was and a connection
of joy hummed easily among the four of us. I can't
think of an evening since then when both weather
and schedules cooperated so well. In the moments
when I worry about our relationship I think back
to that night. I remember the shared joy and fun.

*Staying connected to my teen sometimes means going
with her or his flow: let me see the opportunity when it
presents itself.*

April 25

*No one can escape stress, but you can learn
to cope with it. Practice positive thinking . . .
seize control in small ways.*

~ Adele Scheele

Stress is a part of any life—it's really inescapable, especially so if you are raising teenage children. Emotionally, this is a demanding age. Expectations, decisions, worries, and busy schedules all swirl around us. It's easy to feel overwhelmed, or worse, defeated.

Coping often means breaking stress factors down to manageable levels and then believing that what you need to do will get done. Positive thinking can turn a mountain back into a manageable molehill. We can gently encourage our children in this same way.

Today I will calm down my sense of being overwhelmed by remembering I can do it—and then, I will encourage my teen to do the same if necessary.

April 26

*You do not have to make your children /
into wonderful people. / You only have to remind them / that they are wonderful people.*
·- William Martin

Sometimes as parents we get caught up in thinking there is something we need to do to help shape,
craft, or fine-tune our children. We get caught up in
being over-responsible: a desire to control or fix or
direct these teenagers who are so in the process of
becoming.

Take a deep breath. Relax. For today, just remember how wonderful they are: this is knowledge
you carry within you from the first time you held
them in your arms. It is always there. Be open to an
opportunity to remind them how wonderful they
are. Believe, deeply, in the best of what you know
them to be.

*Today I will quite simply remember the pure wonder at
the heart of who my teenager is.*

April 27

You are a child of the universe, no less than the trees and the stars; you have a right to be here.

~ Max Ehrmann

Some days the job of parenting teens can beat us down, make us feel less than worthwhile. A hard encounter, a conflict, a discouraging choice on the part of our teen can make us feel like we're navigating waters where we are always working against the current.

We may need to take a moment to remember all that is right with our life, and to remember our rightful place on this planet. We belong where we have planted ourselves. We can bloom where we are planted as well, even on the days when the seed is more hidden than visible.

Where I am is the right place to be—I can breathe deep and stand tall in this knowledge. The more fully I know this, the more I model it for my teen.

April 28

What can I do to get my kids to listen . . . ?
The answer is brief: talk less.

         – Nancy Samalin

Many of us know the feeling of "they just don't listen to me." In fact we know it all too well. Many of us, because we don't feel heard, tend to repeat ourselves. But it's a safe bet that if our child didn't listen to us the first time, they won't listen to us the tenth time we say something.

To avoid being tuned out, it's helpful to talk less and to choose your words and issues carefully. Choosing the right moment (or at least the better moment) can also help. There are times and moods when our children are more open. When anyone is overtired, it is not a good time for fruitful conversation or listening.

When I have something to say, I can choose my timing, keep it brief, and expect to be listened to.

April 29

The family [is] the first essential cell of human society.

.- Pope John XXIII

So much of what is learned and lived in their families is integral to who teenagers are as human beings. It's as if family life is the blueprint for other relationships. As parents, we have so much power in the drafting of that blueprint. We lay the foundation and outline the framework.

Whatever our values are, our children absorb them through what we say, how we live our lives, and how we treat others. It's helpful from time to time to think about what our values are, and to reflect on how we express those values. Is a sense of personal joy important to you? Is honesty, creativity, hard work, or discipline?

I will respect the values I want to impart to my child by paying attention to how I live them today.

April 30

You're only here for a short visit. Don't hurry.
Don't worry. And be sure to smell the flowers
along the way.

           ⁓ Walter Hagen

This is such simple advice one wonders why we all need to be reminded of it so often. Most parents struggle with worry at times, and most of us are hurried. Days slip by and we realize we haven't stopped to smell any flowers, enjoy a sunset, or play the piano.

If possible, we need to remember to step lightly upon this planet. Our visit is short; we ought to enjoy it as much as we can. Problems get worked out and worrying never aids the process. There are incredible bounties all around us: our children, their friends, the power and beauty of the natural world, music, painting, our friendships.

Today I will drop the ballast of worry and hurry, breathe
deeply, and smell and taste the gifts that are all around
me.

May 1

Thank you, Mom, for being at all my games.
— A high school senior

We may wait a long time to hear it, but our teens really do need and appreciate our presence in their lives. Sometimes weeks or months can slip by without hearing the appreciation from our children, but believe me, if we aren't there, they really notice the absence.

Attending our children's events whenever we can certainly takes a lot of time. Some days the driving and being there leaves little time for personal activities. Yet it is the accumulation of times we've been there in the audience, celebrating our child's abilities, that builds a steady sense of support. And if we're lucky, our children, from time to time, will thank us.

It's important to be there for my child when I can, and it's enough to know that, even when it's not acknowledged, my presence is appreciated.

May 2

It's easier to go up into the mountains to catch tigers than to ask others for help.

        ·- Chinese proverb

My daughter went through a difficult period during her sophomore year. At that time she was taking ice skating lessons, and every time I handed her over to the care of her coach I felt relieved. Another adult, an adult who loved and cared about her, was taking over.

My daughter was struggling and in need of much emotional bolstering. I often felt inept and inadequate. Whenever she was with her coach or hanging out with the parents of her friends, I felt grateful for the presence of other loving adults in her life.

There are moments when the best we can do is let trusted others care for our child. Today, I will be consciously grateful for these people.

May 3

Imagination was given to man to compensate him for what he is not; a sense of humor to console him for what he is.

— Horace Walpole

It's Monday morning. Again. The kids are getting ready for school. Homework has been misplaced. A specific jacket did not make it into the dryer the night before and your teenage daughter has a few unfriendly words to say about that. Your son informs you at the last minute that he needs cash and you realize you are all out.

There are days when the small things in life go awry and days when bigger problems emerge as well. People often say if they couldn't laugh they'd be crying more. There's a definite wisdom here. When we can laugh at ourselves and at the dilemmas life throws our way, we immediately lighten our load and perhaps heighten our ability to cope.

I can let a sense of humor console me, reminding me that I'm not perfect and that is okay.

May 4

Motherhood is not for the fainthearted. Used frogs, skinned knees, and the insults of teenage girls are not meant for the wimpy.

— Danielle Steele

Sometimes the job of being a parent requires being tough. Being firm. Being unbendable. Most of us have had to dig deep to handle hard-to-look-at injuries. Most of us have had the experience of working hard to stay steady in the face of insults or disdain coming right toward us. Really what that means is not taking too personally what comes at us.

What we need more than anything as parents is that tough inner core that continually realigns itself with what is most important. Is it more important to be right or to be compassionate toward our children? Is it more important to breathe deep and stand for a value or cave in just to be liked in the moment? Parenting demands a rigorous and continual self-awareness, and a toughness to stay on track.

I will consider my job as a parent today, to see where I need to be tough and hold steady.

May 5

Adolescents are travelers, far from home with no native land, neither children nor adults.... Sometimes they are four years old, an hour later they are twenty-five.... There's a yearning for place, a search for solid ground.

-- Mary Pipher

There have been times when I was glad my son was sick, because in the middle of a hands-off phase he wanted me near him. As difficult as these push-pull years are for parents, when our children tend to push us away except when they need certain things, we must remember how difficult growing up can be for them.

There are many moments when the best thing to do is gracefully give our children the space they need. But when the coin flips and they need one of their parents, or a night at home, or to touch base with an old family ritual, do everything you can to be there. It is a moment for them of yearning for a sense of place, of needing to land, if only briefly, on solid ground.

Does my teen need me to gracefully let go or solidly be there today? I will pay attention and see.

May 6

Teenagers open up most naturally late at night, and wise parents take advantage of this reality.

·– Dr. Michael Riera

Studies show that the biorhythms of teens are very different from those of adults. Most teens are night owls, while most parents are dog-tired at the end of the day. But late at night, when things slow down, when kids are finishing homework and unplugging from the computer, they are often more open to conversation than at any other time of day. It is a time of day that lends itself to reflection.

Goodnight rituals are a way of utilizing this time of day. It's not unusual for important questions to emerge if you sit on the edge of the bed, or join your child in a late night snack. It's a good idea to be around, available for such opportunities. The payoff, the moments of connection, are well worth the sleep we might miss.

I will make a point this week of being around in the evenings, or of making goodnight time special in some way.

May 7

*Research shows that the number-one lure
that works on teens in abduction situations
is that of attention/affection.*

– Patty Wetterling

Attention and affection. Two qualities we all need
and we all respond to. In spite of how grouchy teenagers like to pretend they are, they too are hungry for
attention and affection. Examples: a simple brighten-
ing of the face when your teen walks in the door; eye
contact; a caring question like "How did your speech
go today?" followed by time truly taken to listen to
their answer.

Possibilities are endless—a hug, a blown kiss, a
favorite treat in the freezer with their name on it,
lunches (occasionally) made to order with a special
napkin in the paper bag. Attention and affection are
the twin threads that connect us to our children.
Braided together, they create a strong net of support.
Teens most at risk are teens who are missing attention and affection, those whose net is threadbare.

*What simple but important gesture of attention and
affection can I give to my teen today?*

May 8

Teach your children about their heritage.
Encourage them to feel proud of their cultural,
ethnic, and racial identity without feeling
superior.

> ⁓ *What Kids Need to Succeed:*
> *Proven, Practical Ways*
> *to Raise Good Kids*

Even the most mainstream families carry on distinctive traditions. Perhaps it's a song or a joke or special meal. Perhaps it's grace before dinner or a special poem or book at bedtime. Maybe there are characters in your family history that have engendered stories you want to pass on. Celebration of all kinds are filled with opportunities to pass on and teach heritage and tradition.

Being part of a tradition is important to all of us. It gives added meaning to our individual existence to know we're part of a legacy that spans time and generations. It adds meaning and color to our children's lives as well.

Today I will help my children remember they are part of
a noble ancestry and tradition, either by sharing a ritual
or telling a story.

May 9

We find a delight in the beauty and happiness of children that makes the heart too big for the body.

~ Ralph Waldo Emerson

One of the beauties of being a parent is how our children expose us to people and parts of the world we wouldn't know in any other way. Many of my favorite people have come to me through my kids, and participating in their activities has enriched my life in so many ways. When I think of plays I've seen, concerts I've heard, and courage I've applauded on sports teams and at school, I realize how many hidden and unexpected gifts children bring to our lives. As we participate in our children's lives, doors of experience and interest open and blessings spill out into our own.

Today I will reflect on how my children have opened up and filled my life with interesting and fun elements.

May 10

Give me a voice.

.- Search Institute survey respondent

Teens want and need to be heard. They also need to know they matter. We do this first by listening to our teens at home and in the family. But another way teens know they matter is by having opportunities to provide service to others. One of the great things our family's school district has done is require community service of kids starting in middle school and continuing through high school. This provides a chance for older students to return to their elementary school and help younger students with reading or math. Other teens have an opportunity for service through their congregation and are often drawn to programs that serve or feed the homeless.

If our teens are already doing this, we need to applaud and encourage what they are experiencing and learning. If they aren't, we can look around and help them find an opportunity to serve others. A nudge in this direction will always reap benefits.

Today I will pay attention to where my teen is or could be of service to others in our community we share.

May 11

[Teens are] cursed with the pimple-on-the-nose-syndrome. Convinced that there's nothing else anyone will notice, a small blemish can devastate them for days.

·~ Dr. Susan Panzarine

The teen years, especially the early teen years, are an age of painful self-consciousness. Although we may feel impatient, we need to understand that a heightened, and at times obsessive, self-consciousness is a normal aspect of this age. Think of how hard this self-consciousness must be for them, feeling as if they're under a microscope every day.

There really isn't anything we can do to fix or change our children's self-concern. We can hold up to them the mirror of how we see them, which may or may not provide comfort, but more than anything, an ounce of compassion and empathy for this very real part of their development can go a long way.

If my child is struggling with how he or she looks or dresses, I can understand and empathize long before I judge.

May 12

Stay at your center and look beneath the
behavior / to the heart of the child.
　　　　　　　　　　　　　　 — William Martin

In the midst of behavior that angers, disappoints, or concerns us, it can be hard to find our center, let alone stay in it. Behavior, in and of itself, sometimes needs to be concretely dealt with. But if we can steady ourselves—we adults—this will help us see more clearly the forces at work in any given situation.

A teacher calls with a concern about your teen. You can overreact and escalate the problem, or even create a problem where none exists. Or you can calmly approach the concern with both the teacher and your teen. A clearer, wider, more helpful perspective is yours if you can stay sane and centered in the midst of troubling behavior.

Today I will do one thing to bring myself back to center and help me stay there.

May 13

We ourselves must be willing to admit that there is more than one point of view—that our way of seeing things is not the only way.

~ Dr. Rudolf Dreikurs

Some studies show that children come into this world with their own unique wiring. We can see some traits that are genetic, or at least familiar, but no child is a clone. This becomes especially apparent in the teen years. They will surprise us at times (perhaps often) by striding out across the field of their own individuality. "But . . ." we might sputter, taken aback, "I thought you would . . ." or "I thought you said . . . ."

It can be difficult to admit that another point of view or course of action is as worthwhile as ours. Sometimes this is the only appropriate or constructive response on our part. My daughter dyed her hair brown, something I wouldn't have done. Eventually I got used to it and could see it was attractive on her, and that she liked it. Her decision was not what I would have prescribed, but I had to admit it was just as okay.

When and where might I need to be open to my teen's way of doing something, even if it isn't what I would choose?

May 14

If your teen has the courage to report a problem to you, believe him or her, even if what you're hearing seems unimaginable.
— Kathleen Kimball-Baker

In some ways, the world our children are growing up in is unfathomable to us adults. Our teens are exposed to realities of violence, sexuality, and the ravages of drug addiction in ways that would have been inconceivable to us at their age. This happens through the media, the Internet, and in their day-to-day world.

If your child tells you of something or someone who makes them uncomfortable, listen closely. Ask the next question. Don't be hasty in brushing away the unbelievable. If teens have the courage to open up to you, honor that courage by believing them. It's the first and most important step to helping them solve a problem.

I will listen closely to what my teen is telling me today.

May 15

In the parlance of these twelve-step groups,
the recovering addict never wants to let
himself become too Hungry, too Angry, too
Lonely, or too Tired. Any of these states leave
him vulnerable. . . . For teenagers I translate
H.A.L.T. into the quintessential stress-buster.
                                        — Dr. Michael Riera

The H.A.L.T. acronym is a wonderful tool to use
ourselves, and to pass on to our adolescents. When
they feel out of sorts, as if nothing is going right and
they can't do anything right for themselves, this is a
tool they can use for self-examination. Everything
looks and feels worse than it really is under any of
these conditions. It reminds me of the Desiderata
prayer that states, "Many fears are born of fatigue
and loneliness." Sometimes a good night of sleep or
the right phone call can turn a hopeless situation into
a hopeful one.

   We, too, are better parents when we aren't too
hungry, angry, tired, or lonely. These conditions make
any human being more vulnerable.

If someone in the family is struggling today, I or he or
she can put things in perspective by taking a H.A.L.T.
inventory.

May 16

Every mother is a working woman.

·- Anonymous

As parents, we receive many conflicting messages about working outside the home or being at home. Either choice presents its gifts and challenges. The wisdom that is embodied in this slogan is how much wear and tear being a parent entails. One is never "only" a mom or dad.

Quite separate from whatever we do or don't do out in the work world is the honorable work of being there for our children: homework, activities, and the simple acts of paying attention to them. Being a parent is a demanding and honorable path.

For today, I will honor the importance of my job as a parent, which is equal to, if not more important than, anything else I do in this world.

May 17

Most important of all with discipline is that if possible Mother and Father agree, at least about the basic approach.

— Dr. Louise Bates Ames
and Dr. Frances L. Ilg

Sometimes the work of parents is communicating with each other, whether we are married and living together or divorced. In some divorce situations the crevasse is too wide to be crossed. But if at all possible, when dealing with a teen's problems, your position is stronger if you both agree. Single parents often need a good friend, a sounding board, to help discuss and fine-tune their decisions.

Even married people have to work to keep the lines of communication open, to negotiate what seems fair to both. This requires time to talk, listen, and exchange. It's well worth it—the team parenting approach is a strong one.

I will take time to talk over an issue with my partner, my child's other parent, or another caring adult.

May 18

If you watch how nature deals with adversity, continually renewing itself, you can't help but learn.

·– Dr. Bernie S. Siegel

The meadow that erupted in wildfires a year ago is giving birth to an abundance of exquisite, beautiful wildflowers. Water flows around all obstacles, eventually shaping rocks and river banks. The wind lets loose and howls, shaking dead limbs free from trees deep in the forest. The branches that fall become compost for all kinds of new growing things.

No matter how our children might wear us down, wreaking havoc in small and large ways, every bit of the experience can be transformative. Challenges deepen our ability to feel empathy, to connect with others and to open our hearts. The worries and sorrows we run into in parenting connect us with parents all over the globe, now and reaching back in time. We are as resilient as the invisible seeds waiting beneath the roaring flames, ready to open in a calmer time.

No matter what challenges come my way today, I am resilient and ready to be shaped in positive ways.

May 19

A spoken word is not a sparrow. Once it flies out, you can't catch it.

.- Russian proverb

We all run into delicate moments with our teenagers, moments when tempers flare. It is usually in the heat of the moment when people say regrettable things. If we are struggling with our teenagers over an issue that triggers a judgmental response, and we are trying to give them space, those judgments are best left unspoken.

Most of us have a sense of what we don't want to say. Often what helps us keep our tongues silent is the knowledge that once spoken, our words can't be taken back. If words slip out, then we have to work with our regret, we have to work with the mistake of what we said. Once a word flies out, it dynamically changes the air around it.

Is there something I shouldn't say to my teen? Do I need to make amends for something I shouldn't have said?

May 20

Discipline is remembering what you want.
-- David Campbell

Disciplining ourselves to discipline our children can be some of the hard work of parenting. This is the ongoing job of tracking homework, practice, schedules. It is the job of enforcing expectations and consequences. It's the daily job of paying attention.

Because discipline is so much about delayed, earned gratification, we need to find ways to sustain ourselves in the moment, when it may just feel like a grind. It can be most helpful to remember the big-picture view, to remember what goals and desires we and our children are working toward. What it really means is remembering what we want and doing what we need to do today to get there.

When discipline feels difficult, I can always remember the larger picture and feel renewed.

May 21

Our job is not to straighten each other out,
but to help each other up.

·- Neva Cole

When children fall short or wander off course in some way, there's usually a frantic desire to "straighten" them out. Their missteps activate our fear. But while some fear is perfectly sensible and just plain there, consequences or actions based on fear are often not the most helpful.

When it is time to respond and enforce consequences, we want to be centered in the part of ourselves that is ready to do whatever it takes to help our fallen children stand up again; to help our children, who have slipped off the tracks of their goals, get back on track. What we really want to do is bolster and nurture the resiliency of our children.

I will help my child stand stronger today with a smile, a word of encouragement, or a well-thought-out consequence.

May 22

Any kid who has two parents who are interested in him and has a houseful of books isn't poor.

― Sam Levenson

Most of us will hear, probably more than once, how slighted our children feel in comparison to those around them. A child will feel cheated because she doesn't get as many clothes as someone else. Another teen will feel cheated because he didn't go on the exotic spring break trip his friend did.

Occasionally, we parents might be lured into feeling like inadequate providers. But the truth we need to keep coming back to is that a core of caring adults and a passion for learning are the riches that really matter in the long run.

The essence of providing well for my child lies in caring for her or him and encouraging a love of learning.

May 23

True friendship is a plant of slow growth.
- George Washington

Our teens will have struggles from time to time with their friendships. Friends disagree, friends travel apart from each other for periods of time, friends develop different interests, and friends sometimes, often unknowingly, hurt each other. When our children are experiencing shifts in their friendships, often the best thing we can do is listen and guide them as best we can.

Much about friendship reveals itself over time: loyalty, resilience, compatibility. We can gently remind our children that time both heals and reveals. The mark of a good friendship is one where we primarily feel supported and appreciated. We can model this for our teens and gently guide them through the adolescent bumps of friendship.

If my teen is upset about a friendship, I can remind her or him that the strength of any friendship becomes clear with time and experience.

May 24

Ideals are like stars; you will not succeed in touching them with your hands. But like the seafaring man on the desert of waters, you choose them as your guides, and following them you will reach your destiny.

.~ Carl Schurz

If we're lucky, we have people in our children's lives who encourage them to set goals for themselves. Sometimes it's a coach or a mentor or a teacher. But even if we don't have that, we can encourage our teenagers to write down goals for themselves. A seventeen-year-old I know once ran across a list of her goals from two years before. When she realized five out of the seven things on her list were done, a smile spread across her face, a smile of acceptance, pride, and satisfaction.

We can help teens by being aware of their goals and encouraging them to write them down. This is also something we can model by continuously striving for our own goals and ideals.

Today I can encourage my teen to create guiding ideals.

May 25

*In the central place of every heart there is
a recording chamber; so long as it receives
messages of beauty, hope, cheer and courage,
so long are we young.*

— Douglas MacArthur

Beauty, hope, cheer, and courage—these are the things that can keep us going through the time we are raising adolescents. Beauty is always a salve for the weary spirit. Hope tells us that we will find a way every day and that this too shall pass. Cheer helps us see our world from a lighter and brighter perspective. And we all need courage to hold the line, to deal with issues as they arise, and to face what should not be ignored.

These qualities can be nurtured in the center of our hearts by consciously *opening* our hearts to them. Besides keeping us young in spirit, beauty, hope, cheer, and courage give us all the strength we need.

I am ready to embrace beauty, hope, cheer, and courage today.

May 26

*Cherishing children is the mark of a civilized
society.*

-- Joan Ganz Cooney

The teen years can introduce moods and attitudes
that make cherishing a child very difficult. But ultimately it is our job as the mature, loving force in
the family unit to remember what it is about our
teens that we do cherish—even on the days when
this takes conscious effort.

Remember? He's the one who makes you laugh.
She's the one who lights up the household with her
energy. He's the one who is most concerned about
everyone else in the family. She's the one who is
always honest. He is the one who gives hugs easily. She's the one who applauds when anyone in the
family does something brave.

*I will reflect today on what it is about my teen that I
truly cherish.*

May 27

Nothing separates the generations more than music. By the time a child is eight or nine, he has developed a passion for his own music that is even stronger than his passions for procrastination and weird clothes.

-- Bill Cosby

It can be embarrassing to find oneself in the middle of a cliché. But, I have to say, it's happened to me. I find myself wanting to say the same things about my son's music that my father said about mine: it's noisy, it's not very musical, and the lyrics are bad.

What happened? I thought I was cooler than this. Back to the humbling aspect of parenting. Beyond concerns about X-rated lyrics, acceptance can go a long way here. It doesn't hurt to trade musical tastes—alternating one CD of yours for one of your child's. My brother told me that this was an arrangement he made with his kids on road trips. Sounds like a good exchange to me.

With a little grace and a sense of humor, I can share in my child's musical world, or at the very least accept that it is his to enjoy as he wants and needs to.

May 28

*Shared laughter is like family glue. . . . It
brings us together as few other things can.*

·- Valerie Bell

It isn't really possible to *make* funny things happen in
a family, but you can pay attention to its possibility
and make the most of it when it happens. Laughing
together at a joke, laughing together at an absurdity
in the world around you, laughing together over a
shared story with other friends or family members
are all potential sources for shared humor. Pets can
also be a good source of easy laughter.

The great thing about humor is it equalizes everyone, and it's a great connector. Laughing together is
disarming—it exists separately from issues or dis-
agreements. Laughter is simple and genuine.

*Today I will look around for a moment of humor and
be ready to share it with my child.*

May 29

Sometimes things which at the moment may be perceived as obstacles . . . can in the long run result in some good end which would not have occurred if it had not been for the obstacle.

.- Steve Allen

For all of us, our in-the-moment eyesight and our hindsight give very different views of the same picture. As adults, we have probably had the experience of seeing something as a roadblock that later became an opening down a new road. It's an easy lesson to forget and an important one to keep remembering. And the more we remember it and live it, the better we can pass this on to our children.

When we watch our children bump into obstacles, we are much more helpful and hopeful if we can show them the possibility of a new door opening where one has just closed.

Today I can look for the good that can come out of an obstacle in my or my child's path.

May 30

*The last of the human freedoms—to choose
one's attitude in any given set of circumstances,
to choose one's own way.*

— Victor Frankl

An individual moving as a single person through the world will find certain events happen to her or to him. But a parent, who is forever connected to one or more young and growing human beings, is exponentially more often at the mercy of circumstance. Every person in a family adds a layer of complexity and richness to the lives of every other family member.

When the complexity a family member or child brings to the table feels more problematic than anything else, we can choose our outlook. We can whine, feel sorry for ourselves, and cry out, "Why me?" Or we can roll up our sleeves and do what needs to be done, thankful for resources and support available to us.

*I am free today to choose my attitude: let me be drawn
to the light, away from the darkness.*

May 31

Whether kids are 6 or 16, they can enjoy the call of the wild. Make use of whatever green space is available.

— Tenessa Gemelke

Children of all ages respond to what is alive around them. Green parks to run and play in, water that invites you to submerge yourself—these are just two of many possibilities. It is so good to share nature's vibrancy with kids, even if you can only make it happen once in a while.

The other day after dinner my daughter wanted to go out for ice cream. I said sure, if we went inline skating first. So she, my son, and I buckled up our skates and went around a nearby lake. It was a beautiful spring evening. Halfway around it started to sprinkle and near the end an incredible double rainbow appeared. We had a perfect view of the entire spectacle from the lake. It was a magical moment, but it would have been missed entirely if we hadn't been out to enjoy a taste of the wild, together.

I will seize the next opportunity to get my child out into the healing and joyful greenery of nature.

June 1

Children begin by loving their parents. After a time they judge them. Rarely, if ever, do they forgive them.

-- Oscar Wilde

When we are feeling harshly judged by a teenage child, it can help to know we are part of a universal cycle. I know I have never before been at the receiving end of rolled eyes as much as I have while living with a teen.

It's always painful to move from receiving the innocent love and loyalty of a grade-schooler to being raked by the razor-sharp eye of a teen. Yet, occasionally, even the sharpest-eyed teen will slip back into old expressions of affection. Hang on to that—it's a core connection you both hold deep inside, even when it is most dormant.

Today I will pay attention to the most recent gesture of affection from my child. I will let it outshine any criticism or complaints I may have received recently.

June 2

Example is not the main thing in influencing others. It is the only thing.

~ Albert Schweitzer

Whatever values we want to impart to our children, especially to our teenage children, we need to live these values to promote them well. No one sees through that old adage, "Do as I say, not as I do," like a teenager does. Case in point: I recently heard of a teen whose father began drinking after a long period of sobriety. The teen's actual words to his mother were, "If he is going to quit working his sobriety program, why should I have to work mine?"

Modeling is powerful, but we sometimes underestimate its value. If being respectful of others is something we are working on with our teens, we will have much better results if we act as respectfully as we want them to. In so many large and small ways, they pick up values from how we live every day. That is why, as parents, we need to live thoughtful and intentional lives.

What are my intentions and values as a human being and parent? This is what I need to ponder and make sure I am living today.

June 3

Parental intervention can make a significant difference in regard to drinking and driving....
No parent should tolerate it.

~ Dr. Anthony E. Wolf

This is an issue teens need to hear about on a regular basis—some more than others. When to find the right time? Sometimes an article in the newspaper can be a great way to bring up the discussion. Any news reporting on accidents caused by drunk drivers is a good reminder, for ourselves and for them.

It is always our job to protect our children and look out for their best interests. Only harm can come from drinking and driving. It is important that we do everything we can to support them and make this issue crystal clear.

Today I will remind my teen how important it is to not drink and drive, and to never drive with someone who has been drinking.

June 4

*The darn trouble with cleaning the house
is it gets dirty the next day anyway, so skip
a week if you have to. The children are the
most important thing.*

·- Barbara Bush

There's something about the ongoing quality of raising children that is especially apparent in house-cleaning issues. A clean house never lasts very long, and it begs to be taken care of every day. You don't really get to sit back and say, "That's done." And children are forever storming into the house, leaving papers, clothes, jackets, and dirty socks in their wake.

We all have to work it out in the way that is best for us—in terms of what level of tidiness we need, how much we are willing to clean house ourselves, how we negotiate with other family members over this division of labor. Beyond that, for our own sanity, we may need to just let it go. A perfect house is so difficult to attain and impossible to sustain. Instead, go play catch with your son, or a round of tennis with your daughter, or take a walk with your best friend.

As hard as it can be to let go some days, being with my children is more important than how my house looks.

June 5

*Innocence is the knowledge that your child
is yours and yet not yours.*

·— Deepak Chopra

Taking action, letting go. This is the seesaw of parenthood. When our children are young, a lot of action is required of us. As they grow, so does the need to let go of them.

Our children belong to us in the way we feed, clothe, and teach them. But the experiences they have in the world represent the parts of them that do not belong to us. Their challenges, disappointments, hurts, failures, and triumphs belong to them. We can be there, supporting them through it all. But we are not in charge of creating, coercing, or cajoling their life experiences.

Today I will write a list of the things in my child's life I cannot control. Like a dandelion in the wind, I can let go and release them.

June 6

What to say? It is not a bad idea to be honest and simply say "I'm so sorry." If it comes from the heart the children are comforted and relieved that you understand.

— Doris Bodmer

Sometimes it's hard to know what to do or say in the face of a child's disappointment. She's just lost a school election you watched her campaign hard for. He missed the chance to hit a home run at a crucial moment of the game. She gets only a B on a project she slaved over and wanted an A for. His girlfriend just broke up with him and he looks so sad.

Of course we want to save them from these crushing disappointments. It's important to remember that we can't, and that coping with disappointment is a skill everyone needs. As a parent, we can let our child know we understand: empathy is a gift in this moment, even when it doesn't feel like enough.

Disappointment is something I can't fix or take away, but I can let my child know she's not alone with it.

June 7

When you get to the end of your rope, tie a knot and hang on. And swing!

— Leo Buscaglia

This feeling of being at the end of one's rope is not uncommon among people who are raising teens. Teens have a tendency to push us to the very edge of what tethers us. And then, just as we think we can't stand it anymore, something shifts or changes.

Whether our about-to-go-to-college teen is pushing curfews and disregarding our words of wisdom or whether our younger teen's hairdo and preferred dress is driving us crazy, sometimes the best thing we can do is hang on. Tie the knot and hang on. Try swinging, pushing yourself off in a new direction. Or just keep hanging on until the wind shifts, because it will. It always does.

If I'm feeling at the end of my rope, I can trust that hanging on will sooner or later bring me to the fresh winds of change.

June 8

*When I was a boy of fourteen, my father
was so ignorant I could hardly stand to have
the old man around. But when I got to be
twenty-one, I was astonished at how much
he had learned in seven years.*

— Mark Twain

If you're going to be considered less-than-smart or
less-than-astute, it always helps to know you're in
good company. When your child treats you like you
know nothing, you can at least draw comfort from
the fact that many other parents are experiencing
exactly the same thing. It's a general, cultural, and
completely normal trend. But take heart, because at
the other end of adolescence your brainpower and
ability to understand the world will grow exponentially in your child's eyes.

In the meantime, it's not worth trying to convince
any child of how smart you are. It's all in the eyes of
the perceiver. And remember, other people all around
you know how smart and capable you are. Let this
remind you that it's your child's viewing screen that
is askew; there's nothing wrong with your brain.

*Let me hold on to my sense of self, no matter how my
child sees me.*

June 9

*Love is how you stay alive, even after you
are gone.*

— Morrie Schwartz

Most of us bring into our parenting the love of
someone who has gone before us. Perhaps we carry
the gentle love of a father who passed away or the
passionate enthusiasm of a favorite aunt. Perhaps
there was a grandmother known for her wicked
sense of humor and ability to make pies, someone
you think of when you make others laugh or as you
sculpt a peach pie.

The simple yet distinctive way we love our children is how we live on into the next generation as
well. If you have spent hours reading aloud to your
children, they will carry your voice within them. If
you enticed, bribed, or made them practice an instrument they love, then your support will be part
of the joy they'll feel when making music. If you encouraged your children, then part of their courage
will be a gift from you.

I will, with a vibrant aliveness, love my children today.

June 10

*The greatest gift you can give another is the
purity of your attention.*

- Dr. Richard Moss

It's simple and free, and perhaps that is why it so
often escapes our consciousness. When was the last
time we, as the busy parents we are, took time to
give our whole and undivided attention to our teenager? Not just the peremptory question, "How was
your day?" but a space following this query for listening, for asking follow-up questions.

It can happen over a ten-minute breakfast in
the morning, in the evening drive home from soccer practice, or as a late-night snack is being shared.
On our part, what it requires is a momentary clearing of the thousand other details swimming around
inside our brain. Giving undivided attention means
listening and tuning in on multiple levels.

*I will take time today to really pay attention to my
teenager.*

June 11

It's a time of pride at seeing your child develop and mature, but it's also a bittersweet time.

~ Susan Panzarine

As a parent it helps to have friends or a spouse with whom you can share the bittersweet edge of parenting a teen. There is a sadness for the loss of innocence in your child, and the fact that you are needed less is poignant and liberating at the same time.

You watch your child perform in the school play and marvel at this teen who is becoming so much her own person. The next day she is confiding in her friends about something you may or may not ever hear about. There's nothing to do but find consolation when the bitter edge is nipping at you and to fully immerse yourself in the sweetness of watching this interesting and remarkable person emerge.

Bittersweetness is part of this parenting journey. Today I will look for and appreciate the sweetness.

June 12

She, who had no worldly goods to leave, yet left to me an inexhaustible legacy. Inherent in it, this heritage of summoning resources to make . . . courage, hope, resistance, belief.
~ Tillie Olsen

The timeless gifts we give our kids have nothing to do with the expensive jeans they want. The real, sustainable gifts are about modeling ways of being in this world. As intangible as qualities like courage and hope are, we all have a sense of them. And they are built daily in small ways.

Every small gesture in our own lives that exhibits courage and nurtures hope and a belief in the goodness of life not only enriches our lives, but those of our children as well. Remember the gifts handed down to you—strength of spirit, perhaps, or a laughter-filled resilience, or maybe loyalty.

Gestures of courage and hope in my own life make me a better person and parent. I will consciously acknowledge one today.

June 13

Do not ask your children / to strive for extraordinary lives. . . . / Help them instead to find the wonder / and the marvel of an ordinary life. / Show them the joy of tasting / tomatoes, apples and pears.

— William Martin

We often get caught up in coaching and encouraging our children to be all they can be. Understandably so, for we want them to know we believe in them. It's good to balance this energy with contentment in the moment and in the small pleasures in life.

A moment of really enjoying tasty food, or a moment of appreciating the stunning sunset in the sky as you drive to the evening game, is both positive modeling and a way of sharing the good things in life with your teens. Contentment and appreciation of the many ordinary gifts life offers go hand in hand. Moments of contentment feed the voice within us and our children that says, "Life is good. I'm happy to be here."

I will appreciate something utterly ordinary and remarkably alive today with my child.

June 14

Once in a century a man may be ruined or made insufferable by praise. But surely once in a minute something generous dies for want of it.

~ John Masefield

It is easy to notice something positive in our children and not have or take the time to express that. It is also easy to get so busily swept up in our lives that we don't take the time to even notice what our children are doing right.

When a teenager does chores without having to be asked, when a child does something generous for a sibling, when a teen studies hard and does well on a test—these are all opportunities to praise them for a job well done. Praise lets them know they are appreciated, and almost always stokes the fire for future light.

Today I will be expressive of what I appreciate and admire in my teenager.

June 15

*Be glad of life because it gives you the chance
to love and to work and to play and to look
at the stars.*

·- Henry Van Dyke

Every day warrants at least a few minutes of appreciation for life. For most of us there is a lot of joy embedded in loving our children, but it's easy to get caught up in the busyness and forget to focus on the joy. Many of us also find satisfaction in work of some sort, and we find laughter and lightheartedness in moments of play with family or friends.

These qualities create the fullness of life. Sometimes we forget to be consciously grateful for these gifts. And of course a bonus is looking up at the stars or at any of the many amazing and beautiful sights surrounding us. Star-gazing with children is a real treat. It connects us to each other and to the larger mysteries of our planet.

*Today I will pause and be glad for all the gifts in my life
and in the life of my child.*

June 16

A good snapshot stops a moment from running away.

- Eudora Welty

Some people are far better than others at honoring certain moments through photographs. But it is an excellent way for all of us to honor a special memory and to daily hold close to our hearts times of celebration, tenderness, or shared fun.

Photos around the house and on the fridge remind children of all ages that they are important. On a hard day a glance at a photo that captures a proud or happy moment can lighten a heart in an instant. When family members are feeling angry or isolated from one another, a photo of a time when everyone felt close can help present a larger, more encompassing reality. The photos teens put up on their walls tell a story of who and what is important to them.

I can take a moment today to see where a special photo could be added to our collection, as a genuine reminder of joy.

June 17

If you are paying attention, thinking creatively, and maintaining your curiosity, your connection will hold steadfast despite the lack of regular heart-to-heart talks.

— Michael Riera

The sharp drop in direct conversation between parent and teen can be unnerving and worrisome in the adolescent years. We so often worry about what is wrong, forgetting that to a great degree this is normal. But it doesn't have to blind us to the real and potential connection that still remains.

If we pay attention we can make the most of the moments when our child *does* want or need to talk. If we are creative, we can come up with ways to connect by utilizing shared interests or taking up an activity together. And curiosity can be a natural and loving force, as it sparks a genuine interest that can help us ask the next (or the right) question.

Today I will pay attention to where I can and do connect with my teen, even if it's different from how it used to be.

June 18

Man is so made that whenever anything fires his soul, impossibilities vanish.

-- Jean de la Fontaine

Over a hundred years ago the idea of flight was almost inconceivable. The Wright brothers and others were passionately determined to find a way. Just think of what they started and how we now take flight for granted.

In the course of your lifetime, in the course of your children's lifetimes, and in the course of your journey as a parent, there will be moments when you or they think, "That would be impossible." Push yourself a little further each time you hear this. Nothing is impossible if you or your child feels passionately enough. There are creative, inventive, and determined solutions all around you.

Passion and determination can hurl my child and me right over what appears to be an obstacle.

June 19

The capacity to let go, to separate, to allow a child to resolve his or her own destiny, is crucial to being the parent of a teenager. But it is also hard.

— Dr. Anthony E. Wolf

Because letting go and letting our child make her or his own decisions is often so hard, sometimes we need to be very conscious about it. One day my daughter wanted to miss her orchestra rehearsal to do something special with her friends. I didn't think it was a good idea, and for me this was wrapped up in philosophical questions about commitment. But I told her my opinion and then said it was her decision.

Sometimes when I turn a decision like that over to her and let her own it, she makes the choice I want to her make. Sometimes she doesn't. But a year from now when she is at college, she will be making many of these kinds of decisions for herself. She needs to start experiencing them now, as well as the pros and cons, the plusses and minuses that come with each decision.

Today I will think about what area of my teen's life I might need to let go of more, relinquishing my need to control.

June 20

The whole worth of a kind deed lies in the love that inspires it.

— The Talmud

As moms and dads, there are many kindnesses we extend to our children. We drive them places, we provide them with opportunities for learning and fun, we feed them their favorite foods, we welcome their friends into our homes. Most often we do this lovingly.

But at times you might find yourself doing these things resentfully. That's when it's time to slow down and take a little inventory. Are you overtired? Burned out? Feeling in need of a little loving kindness yourself? Figure out what you need to do and make time to take care of yourself. This is the best route back to being inspired by love, rather than bitterness or resentful duty.

If I have wandered away from being inspired by love to do kind deeds, I can find my way back today.

June 21

*Make a real effort to put a winning spin on
who you are. . . . It makes a difference.*
— Pamela Espeland

Teens need encouragement to do this on a regular
basis. As parents, we can often point this out and
encourage them and help give them the language to
see themselves in a better light. If you catch your
teen saying, "I wish I played the saxophone as well
as John does," you can point out what he is good at,
or how far he has come in playing the saxophone in
just a short amount of time.

We can consciously help them turn around how
they look at themselves. And we can model this by
how we talk about and see ourselves as well. *Seeing*
oneself as capable and successful is key to *being* capable and successful.

*Today I will consciously see myself and my child in a
positive light.*

June 22

*One of the oldest human needs is having
someone to wonder where you are when you
don't come home at night.*

·- Margaret Mead

As much as teens moan and groan about curfews,
the saddest and loneliest teens are the ones who
don't have anyone who cares about when they come
home. It is an ancient need to have loved ones know
where you are and when you are returning, who care
about your safety.

Beneath the curfew issue is this motivating impulse: to know where our children are and to know
that at a reasonable, agreed-upon hour they will
return home safely. So, no matter what issues may
arise in our homes, and curfew is a common one,
we can remember that having one, and enforcing
one, is an ancient and needed connection.

*Today, in spite of any arguments about curfew, I can
remember that my child really does want to know that
I would notice if he or she did not come home.*

June 23

The first duty of love is to listen.

.- Paul Tillich

Sometimes I learn a lot from listening to my son and his friends. Car pools are great for this. But sometimes I will ask him a question and then only half listen to his response.

Listening is an underrated skill in our culture. Listening requires an emptying out of our own needs, our desire to talk, and our thinking patterns. It requires being in the moment, not worrying about the next event. Our children deeply need to be listened to, just like we do.

Today I will listen, clearly and deeply, to what my child is saying to me and to the world.

June 24

Men are slower to recognize blessings than misfortunes.

~ Livy

Intellectually, I know I should count my blessings. But so often I forget to. One sure way to remember is to be around people who are struggling in concrete and palpable ways. When I watch someone walk with what looks like a painful limp, I realize how fortunate I am to be able to move my body without pain.

When my son and I served dinner for the homeless, he said to me, "We are really lucky that we always have food to eat." People who have lived through poverty or wartime are often conscious on a daily basis of their good fortune in having food and shelter. The ability to count blessings helps us appreciate our own lives and pass on a sense of gratitude to our children.

I will count my blessings today and encourage my child to do the same.

June 25

If you want your children to improve, let them overhear the nice things you say about them to others.

~ Dr. Haim Ginott

It's a psychological truth that we human beings respond positively to praise. Once complimented, we aim to please even more. The same is true of our children. So often however, we might think to describe them glowingly to someone else but forget to tell them directly.

Take time once in a while to say out loud what it is you admire in your child. Notice and talk about where he or she has grown or taken risks. Admire the ways in which your child works hard. Forget for the moment your desire to improve your child and celebrate who and what she or he is today. Coincidentally, it is often this kind of praise that makes your child want to continue to improve herself or himself.

I will take time today to talk about my child's good qualities.

June 26

It is important to be heroic, ambitious, productive . . . but the soul has different concerns, of equal value: downtime for reflection, conversation, and reverie. . . .
— Thomas Moore

Our culture tends to reward outward signs of ambition and success. Because we want our children to do well, we sometimes focus on tangible results and overlook the inner soul. That's when problems like addiction or depression can surface. Our overall well-being depends upon caring for our souls a little each day.

The nourished soul can persevere through long periods of discipline and work. Reflection is important; so is conversation with loved ones. Immersing oneself in the beauty of a starry sky or a blossoming tree can provide inspiration for days to come. So carve out time for your children to do homework, but also remember to honor the time they spend laughing with friends or playing basketball or painting at the easel—these are the less tangible but oh-so-important soul-times.

I'll make time to feed my soul today, and I will honor my child's desire to do the same.

June 27

Raising children is a creative endeavor, an art, rather than a science.

.- Dr. Bruno Bettelheim

Every child's personality, talents, drives, needs, and desires are unique. A strategy or motivation that works great with one child can fall completely flat with another. Children are constantly changing, too, so that a process that works well today can be useless a month from now.

That is why raising children challenges us so. It is not a predictable or quantifiable experience. No, it is a way of life that works best if we lean into our intuitions and are willing to try creative solutions when problems arise. Thinking outside the box is a real asset for a parent, because of course our children are experts at drawing outside the lines. Sometimes we need to meet them there.

Where in my parenting do I need to apply my intuition and creativity?

June 28

Hope is the thing with feathers / That perches in the soul.

— Emily Dickinson

Feeling hopeless about a certain aspect of your teenager? That the room will never get cleaned, that the paper won't be written, that she'll never break up with her lazy boyfriend? It's easy to fall into hopeless thinking, whether the issues are small or large.

But hope is that quiet bright light within us. It's the feathered part of us that wants to take wing, believing in all good things and knowing anything is possible. This part lies quietly inside, and we can access it intentionally.

Today I will dig deep into my soul and feel the hope that is there—hope for my teen and hope for myself.

June 29

Talking with one another is loving one another.
- Kenyan proverb

"When a child feels like talking, drop everything," my friends and I always say. Simple conversation is at the cornerstone of connection between loved ones. Of course our teens won't always want to talk when we want them to, but it's always worth the effort on our part to ask. We can ask how their day went, or how a specific test we knew of went. We can ask about the friend who broke her leg last week. We can ask about a particular activity. Or, what did they like about the movie they just saw or the book they just read?

Sometimes if we ourselves have news to share, that can be a good way to open a conversation. As simple as it is, such give and take is an important vehicle for a loving and vibrant connection. And it can happen anywhere: in the car, on a shared trip to the neighborhood coffee shop, over dinner.

Today I will take time to talk to my teen, to share who we are.

June 30

*The word "no" carries a lot more meaning
when spoken by a parent who also knows how
to say "yes."*

·~ Joyce Maynard

It requires a series of light adjustments to keep an airplane on its course. Of course, the weather affects how a plane needs to be steered. Parenting also requires a delicate balance between yes and no. Parenting is affected by the emotional weather of adolescents; many winds are blowing through the teen years.

Taking into consideration the emotional weather report and the many forces at work in the world of raising teens, it is wise to carefully choose our nos and to say yes when we can. A balance provides a chance for us to be on the same glidepath with our children, on our way to a successful and safe landing.

Let me carefully and thoughtfully choose my noes and balance them out with loving yesses.

July 1

A family vacation is one where you arrive with five bags, four kids and seven I-thought-you-packed-its.

— Ivern Ball

Family vacations often require a lot of extra work on the part of the parents. No matter how long it is or how far you go, there are bound to be things you forgot and problems you didn't predict. Vacations tend to challenge the family unit in new ways.

Yet trips and traveling as a family are often important bonding times. Even if things go wrong, for this period of time you are an island, away from the usual pressures of peers. There is a clear message embedded in traveling together that says family is important—important enough to carve out this time together and make special plans and arrangements. Kids often remember these trips fondly.

Time together as a family, even simple trips, is always worth the extra effort. I will remember today how this time together creates lasting memories.

July 2

The attitudes about sexuality and family life that are transmitted nonverbally are more powerful than books or classes.

— Janice Presser

Talking about issues of sexuality with our teens is of course important. But our own attitudes and feelings about sexuality also have a significant impact. This calls for self-awareness: what are our values and what do we want to pass on to our children?

The same is true for family life. If we say family time is important but we are always at work and rarely available, guess what children learn at a deep level? On the other hand, if we regularly make time for kids and family, they learn that this time is valued and valuable.

Today I will look closely at my attitudes about sexuality and family life: what am I really passing on?

July 3

My daughter's adult friends, perhaps without even knowing it, helped me realize that as a parent, I truly did not and do not have to go it alone. I don't have to be all things at all times.

-- Kathleen Kimball-Baker

My son's friend has a dad who often takes a group of the guys skiing. We tend to take my son and his friends to musical or theater events. When my daughter's best friends are strapped for a car or a ride, they sometimes call on me and I always get a kick out of this.

A neighborhood mom helped my daughter search online for scholarship opportunities. Another neighborhood mom, knowing my son would love it, dropped off a ski hat her son no longer wanted. In small and large ways, the other adults my kids know add so much to their lives, and every gesture lightens the load on my shoulders.

Today I will appreciate how much other adults help my children, and me as well.

July 4

*Nature's peace will flow into you as the sun-
shine into the trees. The winds will blow their
freshness into you, and the storms their energy,
while cares will drop off like autumn leaves.*

— John Muir

Exposing our children to the healing power of nature is a gift, one that can tide them over throughout their entire lives. Sometimes the sun on our
cheeks is the kindness a person needs to get through
a hard day. A walk near trees in the autumn or near
the lapping water of rivers or lakes can soothe like
nothing else. A wind blowing out of the cold north
or from the balmy south can refresh our thoughts
in ways that words sometimes can't.

As parents, we can provide places for and an
awareness of the healing power of nature. Perhaps
we have a special family place near water or woods.
Or we might have a favorite city walk that passes
by trees, flowering bushes, or a small stream. We can
help provide these experiences for our teens.

*Let me remind my teen of the healing power of a sun-
set or a brisk wind, in part by absorbing and appreciating these things myself.*

July 5

True fear as part of child-raising may bring better behavior at home, but overall it produces less kind and considerate humans. Without fear as leverage, parenting is harder.

.- Dr. Anthony E. Wolf

Many of us have lived through a cultural shift: parenting power used to come from inspiring fear in children; nowadays, we are trying to find more positive ways to motivate and move them. Sometimes we may long for the old leverage, the old kind of power that allowed no room for discussion. Today we tend to talk things through, to engage our teens in a two-way dialogue.

Talking through conflicts and life's big issues with our teens requires more of our time and thoughtfulness than does simply using threats. If this feels hard, it's good to remember that our careful modeling is all a part of raising kids who know how to listen and consider the needs of others.

I can find creative and acceptable ways to work with my teen without resorting to the use of fear as leverage.

July 6

Stress is basically a disconnection from the earth, a forgetting of the breath. . . . It believes that everything is an emergency. Nothing is that important.

·- Natalie Goldberg

Not only is this important for us as parents to remember, but it's an important lesson to model and pass on to our children. A certain amount of stress exists in the lives we lead. But when we react to stress by becoming overly anxious and forgetting to calm ourselves, we make things seem worse than they really are. Of course we all do this from time to time. But this kind of heightened stress creates bad tempers, makes us say and do things we regret, and pulls us out of the present moment.

It can help to breathe deeply, to slow down, to realize what is not an emergency. A demanding life can be faced and lived much more easily from a calm and centered state. If you live this, you can begin to teach it to your children.

In the face of high stress I can breathe deeply, re-center myself, and realize nothing is as unmanageable as it seems.

July 7

*One of the things I learned the hard way
was that it doesn't pay to get discouraged.
Keeping busy and making optimism a way
of life can restore your faith in yourself.*

·– Lucille Ball

Lucille Ball was one of the first women involved in the business side of Hollywood. After the dissolution of her marriage and business partnership, she figured out a way to run her company alone and be successful at it. She had to reinvent herself and her career. It would have been easy to become discouraged, to give up. Instead, she excelled.

It can be easy for any of us to become mired in the mud of disappointments. To spin our wheels, feel bad, go nowhere. The idea that planting and cultivating optimism can restore faith in oneself is inspiring. When disappointment does come, it is probably best to feel it and let it go, like blossoms falling off a tree. And then return to, nurture, and nourish whatever optimism you have.

I can restore faith in my life by planting and watering every seed of optimism in my life.

July 8

Yes, there is a Nirvana; it is in leading your sheep to a green pasture, and in putting your child to sleep, and in writing the last line of your poem.

- Kahlil Gibran

A friend of mine whose daughter spent a night in the hospital due to alcohol poisoning spoke of how in the following weeks, every night when she crawled into bed and both of her children were settled in bed or inside for the night, she felt a sense of peace descend. Everyone was home. Everyone was safe.

Brushes with crisis can remind us of the simple gifts of being together, of being alive, and of doing our work, whatever it is. Our teens come home to sleep at night. Our children are doing their homework. We ourselves have work to do. Everyone will be home for dinner tonight. These are the simple gifts that, properly cherished, can feel close to nirvana.

What simple gifts of life with my teen do I need to cherish and honor today?

July 9

Children have things on their minds too.
Perhaps that is why they sometimes don't
behave as they wish they would.

⌐ Esther Davis-Thompson

If a teen's behavior disappoints us, there's a good chance our teen is also disappointed. Perhaps he went back to a crowd he knows isn't good for him and got arrested at a party. Maybe she was sick and insisted on taking her test anyway and did poorly. Maybe she turned down a babysitting job, even though she owes you money, because a certain boy might ask her out.

Teenagers have a lot on their minds. Socially, every day is full of shifts and swings. And then there's the impact of hormones on their moods. With every activity and every class there is pressure to keep up and to perform. We don't need to excuse less-than-constructive behavior, but it can help to understand how much they are balancing and trying to figure out.

When my teen acts in disappointing ways, I can ask
and consider if it's the way he or she wished to act.

July 10

*Family faces are magic mirrors. Looking
at people who belong to us, we see the past,
present and future. We make discoveries
about ourselves.*

— Gail Lumet Buckley

As imperfect as they are, family connections are ones that last forever. The people we live with, day in and day out, know us in ways that no one else does. In this way, family life is the crucible of self-knowledge and self-learning. The people we live with reflect back to us who we really are.

When we see our children change, mature, and grow, we get to reflect that back to them. If you find there is some part of yourself that keeps running into a brick wall with your child, it's an opportunity to take a look at yourself and perhaps change a way of thinking or acting that no longer works for you. Being a parent is like being on a voyage of self-discovery: as soon as you get one phase figured out, a new one arrives.

I can appreciate today how family life sharpens and hones my sense of self.

July 11

*The most called-upon prerequisite of a friend
is an accessible ear.*

.- Maya Angelou

We teach our children about friendship by sharing
friendship qualities with them and through modeling
our own friendships. There are many elements that
go into friendship—the ability to have fun, to share
interests, and to be there for each other, to name a
few. But the ability to listen to each other is key.

If your child knows he or she can talk to you
and you will lend an ear, you are modeling a cornerstone of friendship. The same is true when your
child sees you listening and talking to your friends.
Friendship makes the world a much warmer place.
The ability to make and keep friendships is one
worth fostering—in ourselves and in our children.

Today I will be a good friend by taking time to listen.

July 12

Welcome and accept / children as they are.
— William Martin

So often our teens need to know we cherish what is special about them. Does your child who drives you crazy in many ways have the gift of making you laugh? Do you let him know often how that brightens your life? Is your daughter—the whirlwind, the white tornado—also the one who makes events special in your home, who knows how to celebrate important moments? Do you let her know how important that is to all of you? Is one of your children— the one who is hard to motivate—also the one who is kind and sensitive? Do you thank her or him regularly for that quiet thoughtfulness?

What part of my teen do I need to accept and welcome today?

July 13

*There must be quite a few things a hot bath
won't cure, but I don't know many of them.*
·- Sylvia Plath

We all need curing or healing sometimes. No matter how we might strive for happiness, no matter how well things may be going, we all have our down days, our moments of sadness or low energy. No use fighting it or feeling inadequate because of it. Rather, it's good to remember that it's okay and very human to have such days.

It's also human to need to comfort oneself on such days. A hot bath, especially with a candle lit in the room, never fails to comfort me and most people I know. Water of all kinds is comforting and transforming: a boat ride or vigorous swim can also work wonders. The swirling demands of parenthood can take a break while we rejuvenate and heal ourselves in a small and simple way.

*Today I can take time to comfort and heal myself, even
with something as simple as a candlelit bath.*

July 14

*Drag your thoughts away from your troubles
by the ears, by the heels, or any other way,
so you can manage it; it's the healthiest thing
a body can do.*

— Mark Twain

It's a good thing to take a break from what is wrong in our lives and look toward what is right. Troubles tend to draw us in—for one thing, they are often more dramatic than the rest of our everyday lives. For another, many of us have a tendency to over-think problems. But taking a break from problems can be enormously refreshing and productive. This is one reason why vacations are good for the spirit: just taking a break from the grind of daily life reminds us of how winged our spirits can be.

If we as parents dragged ourselves away from focusing on what is wrong with our teens, what we need to figure out or fix, we might free ourselves to see the things they do that are so right and wonderful and uniquely them.

Today I will turn my thinking away from any troubles with my child or our relationship to what is right and worthy of noting and celebrating.

July 15

A helpful role that parents can play is to remind—actually tell—their teenage child that all that goes on in the electronic world is not always real.

 ⌐ Dr. Anthony E. Wolf

Just a generation ago people would have been astounded at the major role electronics play in the lives of our children. We used to work to set limits with the TV, but now there are the added attractions of the Internet, computer games, e-mail, cell phones, instant messaging, and so on. Teens can easily be "plugged in" all of their waking hours.

As parents we need to limit some of this, or find other ways to keep them involved with the world. A child who is getting good grades, has friends, and is involved in an athletic or artistic interest probably doesn't have time to overuse electronics. A quieter, shyer, less involved child might be more at risk for this. As parents, we need to figure out what our family rules or guidelines are in this area. Time needs to be saved for human interaction, too.

Where is my child's usage of electronics at right now? If I am uneasy with it, I will look to see if he is balancing electronics with studies, friends, and family time.

July 16

Make your home a warm and inviting place
for all family members—somewhere your
kids want to be.

> *— What Kids Need to Succeed:*
> *Proven, Practical Ways*
> *to Raise Good Kids*

If you don't already have a room or space in your house where your kids like to hang out, you can create one. Your kids can even be part of planning a room that is inviting to them and their friends. Another way to make your house inviting is to stock favorite snack foods. But best of all, a friendly and welcoming face and atmosphere goes a long way to making children want to be at your house.

There are days when you might miss having more quiet and space, but the huge advantage is knowing where your children are and knowing they are safe. This benefit truly outweighs any inconvenience. Another positive side effect is getting to know your child's friends, and getting to know your child *as* a friend—all positive connections to make as a parent.

I will welcome any opportunity for my child and friends
to come for dinner or to just hang out.

July 17

Too long a sacrifice / Can make a stone of the heart.

— W. B. Yeats

Sometimes parents allow themselves to become completely burned out by the demands of their children. To some extent we are all at risk for this. The danger here is in turning our hearts to stone, thereby dulling the edge of parent-child love in a way that is very hard to recover from.

When the word "sacrifice" comes to mind it bears reflecting upon. Is it time to scale back on what you do for your child? Is it time to more consciously balance it with what you do for yourself?

I will do one thing today to keep my heart from hardening.

July 18

I guess what I've really discovered is the humanizing effect of children in my life—stretching me, humbling me.

— Susan Lapinski

Children stretch us in so many ways—emotionally, physically, financially, just to name a few. They expose us to activities and people we would never meet otherwise. Many of these people and experiences enrich us. Think of the music concerts you might not have heard or the team events you might not have witnessed or participated in. Think of the tender and humorous moments your children have brought to you.

Just as children widen and broaden our world, so do they often humble us. Even a company CEO can be easily leveled by her or his teenager. Hard as it is to take, this too is good for our souls.

Today I will appreciate how my child brightens my world and also keeps me grounded.

July 19

Hearts like doors open with ease when you say "thank you" and when you say "please."
·– Mary Jo Copeland

Once in a while we need to remind ourselves to reach back and touch the basics. It may be called "manners," or "polite behavior," but embedded in it is a sense of respect between human beings.

Sometimes as parents we bark orders. Sometimes teens bark orders at us. Sometimes things are said in the heat of the moment that really hurt. Whoa. Stop. Throw the red flag up. Do not get lulled into acting out or accepting disrespectful behavior, because it never feels good on the receiving end.

I will be conscious today of how I ask my teen to do something. I will treat her the way I want her to treat and talk to me.

July 20

*The best inheritance a parent can give his
children is a few minutes of his time each day.*
— O. A. Battista

These are simple and powerful words. They are also
easily forgotten words. Most of us do live in an ac-
celerated world: our lives are filled with schedules,
events, work, and other responsibilities. Sometimes
our brains are so focused on the to-do lists that we
forget a huge priority in our lives: our kids.

Even a small, simple, but focused time with our
children is a great way to connect. Riding in the
car together. A visit in the kitchen before bedtime.
A middle-of-the-day phone call. All of these are
simple ideas, but the act of giving our children a
few minutes of undivided time is a way to see and
feel how they are doing. This focused attention feeds
the connection between parent and child.

*I will take a few minutes today to do something simple
yet special with my teen.*

July 21

If children are to learn to give up an absolute insistence on having their own way, so must their mothers.

-- Elaine Heffner

Who among us doesn't want to be right all of the time? Yet, if we are honest, this is a difficult quality to live with. And many of us are stubborn in ways that can prevent discussion or listening. One of the keys to relationships of all sorts is this ability to give and take, to listen to one another.

If we are trying to teach a teen that she can't have it her way all the time, we need to be aware of this desire in ourselves. Sometimes I will fixate on how things ought to be, and I will push for it. But often, if I listen to my teen, she may have very good reasons for doing things her way. Working things out requires openness rather than an insistence on one person getting her or his way.

If I'm being stubborn, I can listen and see if it feels right to give and take in this situation.

July 22

Children may close their ears to advice, but may open their eyes to example.

·- Anonymous

There is a huge part of parenting that isn't about what you do for your child, or what you tell her or him to do. It's about how you live your own life. If you want your child to have dreams and goals, you might want to look at your own dreams and goals. If you expect your child to be honest, it's important to take an inventory of your honesty level. You expect your child to be an enthusiastic learner—when was the last time you read a book or took a class or learned a new skill?

How you live your life and who you are as a human being has a significant impact on what your child learns and absorbs from you.

I will be thoughtful today about what I want to teach my child and what I want or need to do to model that.

July 23

I think a hero is an ordinary individual who finds strength to persevere and endure in spite of overwhelming obstacles.

— Christopher Reeve

Most of us are far more ordinary than we perhaps want to admit. Either that or we are so aware of our ordinariness that we don't feel at all heroic. Yet heroic and ordinary can be braided together to form quietly courageous people.

As parents we will run into obstacles in our own lives. People lose jobs, lose a loved one, make the difficult decision to divorce, struggle with addiction. Add our children's obstacles to that mix, and we will feel compelled to help them navigate their way through. To simply persevere, to keep getting up in the morning and doing the best we can when times are tough, to dig deep and be strong for ourselves and for our children, makes us quiet heroes.

Today I will acknowledge the courage and strength it takes to persevere in this ordinary life of mine.

July 24

*Innocence is the knowledge that you can
guide children but never control them. . . .
In innocence, this fact can be accepted with
a peaceful heart.*

-- Deepak Chopra

There are travel guides, tour guides, activity guides, spiritual guides. A guide is often one who gently holds out what is possible in front of the traveler. A guide is one who often models and shares previous experiences and hard-won wisdom. Sometimes a guide communicates expectations. Always, good guides encourage those under their care.

Today I need to remember my job as a guide. It's a job that requires gentleness and honesty. Where might I need to point out a fork in the road ahead to my teen? Where might I need to encourage him to use his gifts more? Where might I need to step in and let her know I am disappointed by her choice? When I think of myself as my child's guide and rely on my intuition, what kind of guidance does my teen most need right now?

I will ponder this question and act when I'm clear about what I most need to do as a guide.

July 25

The universe is full of magical things, patiently waiting for our wits to grow sharper.
-- Eden Phillpotts

The universe is a great teacher, one that can help us parents immensely. It is full of treats: surprises, serendipity, gifts. On some days this is easier to see than on others. But what if it's all in *how* we see, all in what we are looking for and paying attention to?

My teen talks to me about quitting piano lessons, which I don't want him to do, and moments later his teacher calls and asks him to perform a special song at the next recital. He is flattered and agrees to stick with it for a while longer. My daughter falls in love with her instrument through a chance encounter with a master musician in the field. Playing it opens many wonderful and surprising doors for her.

I will notice and point out to my teen how the universe works in amazing, even magical, ways.

July 26

*I know why families were created, with all
their imperfections. They humanize you.
They are made to make you forget yourself
occasionally, so that the beautiful balance
of life is not destroyed.*

— Anaïs Nin

Families are where kids learn to be honest, to be empathetic, to be kind, to be who they really are, and to work out differences. Living with others is always an exercise in sharing—everything from the bathroom to a favorite chair to what's left in the refrigerator.

As parents, the atmosphere we create and the behavior we model helps shape our kids. If we want children who can be team members, who can be honest and fair in their negotiations out in the world, it all starts at home. If we can accept our own flaws and our children's flaws with a sense of humor and a measure of forgiveness, we will be creating a humane and balanced home, rather than a judgmental one.

*I can appreciate today how family life humanizes me,
keeping me real, humble, and balanced.*

July 27

Adolescence is perhaps nature's way of pre-
paring parents to welcome the empty nest.
― The Good Stepmother:
A Practical Guide

Teenage-hood has something in common with the
last month of pregnancy: It becomes so burden-
some and uncomfortable that even the most reluctant among us begins to feel ready for the next
phase. A teen who is constantly stretching rules and
boundaries can help a parent see the beauty in his
soon being out on his own, stretching other rules
and boundaries.

Of course many of us feel mixed about this process of living together for eighteen years and then
suddenly being apart. Feelings of loss, of missing
all of this challenge and fullness, loom ahead. We
are both preparing, and sometimes that preparation
hurts.

Preparing ourselves for separate lives can create a pain-
ful dissonance, but today I will simply appreciate this
amazing, complicated process.

July 28

Give up the role of manager and get yourself rehired as the consultant to your teenager's life. From this perspective, more to the side than face-to-face, parents have tremendous influence.

— Michael Riera

One of the transitions so difficult for us parents, especially in early adolescence, is getting fired from the role of managing many of the details in our kids' lives. This role was so important in their early years and oh, we felt so needed. The shift requires effort, openness, and letting go, and ultimately entails some sadness.

But if we can be aware of the need for this switch, it is possible to adjust to a new and more indirect role. As a consultant we can be there to answer questions when they are asked and to point out choices rather than make them. Consultants are often called in on an as-needed basis. For this, we need to be open, available, and alert to opportunities.

I will do everything I can today to be an available and helpful consultant, leaving behind my desire to take over as manager.

July 29

A journey of a thousand miles begins with a single step.

         ~ Chinese proverb

Something you need to do soon with regard to your child? Is it making a phone call? Setting up an appointment? Having that tough conversation? Is there something you need to do to take care of yourself, something that, if ignored, might interfere with your sense of serenity?

Part of the delicate balance of parenting is taking care of ourselves and our children. Both are big jobs, especially alongside the other jobs most of us juggle. When it feels like too much, it's time to take a deep breath, and remember that all journeys are composed of small steps.

What small step would bring me more peace of mind today? I will figure that out and then take it.

July 30

You never can be quite sure if you'll be dealing with Jekyll or Hyde when your child walks through the door.

~ Susan Panzarine

Part of the roller coaster of teenage hormones is moodiness. Your previously happy-go-lucky child may still surface from time to wonderful time, but there's also this new being who's entered her or his body. A being that can be irritable, sarcastic, and barely able to respond in monosyllables to your oh-so-interested questions.

It's tough on parents, this change and unpredictable quality. Gone are the emotionally simpler days of those younger years. It helps to know we are in good company, that this is happening in many homes and most of the time is a perfectly normal part of teenage development. If it's tough on us, we need to remember how tough it is for them.

As much as these changes may surprise or sadden me, I can embrace the bumpy parts of the road as a necessary step in my child's passage toward adulthood.

July 31

*Flowers always make people better, happier
and more helpful; they are sunshine, food
and medicine to the soul.*

— Luther Burbank

When I was teaching writing classes to teenagers, they loved to write about a favorite flower or tree in their yard, or in a grandparent's yard. As immune as teens sometimes seem to innocence around them, we need to remember that the scent of a lilac tree and the beauty of fresh roses on the table are things they appreciate, too.

An easy way to bring sunshine into family life is by growing flowers, appreciating the gardens in your neighborhood, or having some at the dinner table once in a while. Flowers, outside or inside, bring a ray of sunshine into everybody's day. It's a simple way of saying that today is special because we are here for it.

Today I will nurture and brighten my day and my family's day with flowers.

August 1

The only way to bring peace to the earth is to learn to make our own life peaceful.

~ The Buddha

It's easy to get caught up in causes that exist outside of us, and often it's important. But working for peace out in the world when our own lives are far from peaceful is an exercise in futility, and often a practice of distraction or escape. If we cannot practice at home what we preach in the larger world, then there's an emptiness to our words and actions.

Teenagers are looking for, and can send a piercing gaze through, this kind of hypocrisy. That is part of how our children help keep us honest. It's a worthy challenge: to match our inner and outer lives, to match our aspirations for the world with what we need to work on at home.

I will do one thing today to make our home life more peaceful: slow down, share a laugh with my child, bake a cake, or give everyone a loving hug.

August 2

*In all the years I've been a therapist I have
yet to meet one girl who likes her body.*

— Mary Pipher

As parents of teenage girls, we need to remember
how hard the body image issue is for most of them.
Genuine compliments that don't focus on stereo-
typical standards of beauty can be valuable: when
you notice they look especially alive or that a certain color highlights their eyes, take the time to be
generous and say so. Concerns about how they are
dressed do need to be stated, but in a manner that
emphasizes the clothes, not their bodies. Girls are
so easily defensive about how they look that any
negative comment or look can contribute to their
self-consciousness.

Anything we can do to contribute to our daughters' overall physical health, such as good nutrition
at home and support for their physical activities,
will help them feel better about their bodies.

*Today I will do one thing to contribute positively to my
daughter's body image, either by complimenting her,
feeding her a healthy meal, or exercising with her.*

August 3

*Kids who feel alienated from their families
often discover aspects of deep kinship during
a family trip, levels of connection that had
previously gone undetected.*

·~ Michael Riera

There is a lot to be said for packing the family unit
into a car or other mode of travel and leaving the
familiar routine behind. It's like putting a protective
wreath around yourselves. As a unit you go explor-
ing together. The usual roles and expectations get
mixed up, and everyone gets to see a slightly different aspect of themselves and each other.

Not long ago we veered off the road on a side trip
to see a waterfall. Behind the waterfall was a huge
sand dune. My son began to climb it, then my husband and I did as well. My son was a much faster
and more agile climber than either of us. At the top
he beamed and said he wished his sister was with us.
"She would love this!" he announced. I was touched
by the level of connection I felt among the three of
us, and even with our missing family member.

*Whether it's a small trip or a large trip, I can enlist my
family in planning some special time together.*

August 4

Monitor your conversations / for a seven day period. / Make a note each time / that you complain or blame.

— William Martin

Before I started a diet once I kept track of what I ate for seven days. It was an eye-opener. It turned out that I ate many things unconsciously, especially small snacks I never really "counted." Keeping track gave me a new awareness, which was hard to take at first but in the long run proved very helpful.

How we talk to our children is another part of our lives in which it is easy to be unconscious. What we don't like to hear in them we may need to watch for in ourselves. How much do we complain or blame others? From time to time we all may need to monitor how we talk to family members, especially if we're feeling displeased with how they talk to us.

When it comes to tone of voice or attitude today, I will keep track of my own words and actions.

August 5

I think the next best thing to solving a problem
is finding some humor in it.

— Frank A. Clark

Sometimes when a life dilemma feels unsolvable, the best solution is to have a sense of humor. Humor gives us space but also lightens the burden. Humor acknowledges the presence of something difficult but says, "I'm not going to let this get me down, I will keep putting one foot in front of the other."

Sometimes problems are about what we can't change in another family member. Sometimes we are asked to deal with what feels like a big lesson in loss. Sometimes it's a little bad luck throwing an obstacle into our day. Whatever the current scenario is, if at the end of the day you can't think of a solution, then allow yourself to see the humorous thread. Teens are often particularly great at pointing out the humor in life.

No matter what today's problem is, I can love my life and teen with a sense of humor.

August 6

We love because it's the only true adventure.
— Nikki Giovanni

The word "adventure" brings to my mind images of mountain trails, peaks with panoramic views, canoes moving through whitewater rushes, rugged terrain, and hard-earned yet incredibly beautiful views.

Certainly loving a teenager challenges our hearts in ways that the most rugged terrain can challenge mind and body. Whether we are climbing a steep peak at the moment with our teen, or skating close to a precipitous edge, or putting one foot in front of the other in a low oxygen, high-altitude zone, we can rest assured that somewhere out there is a view, a resting place that will make the trip well worth it.

Love's adventure is filled with challenging terrain, moments of beauty, and an ongoing deep aliveness.

August 7

Opportunity's favorite disguise is trouble.
— Frank Tyger

When trouble comes knocking at our door, most of us groan. Nobody wants the bother of it. It might be the news of low grades at school or the coach's report that a bad attitude is creeping in or a disagreement with a teacher or teen whose moods can slice a dark hole into everyone else's day.

Behind the trouble is an opportunity. Perhaps it's an opportunity to talk about your teen's inner emotional life. Perhaps it's an opportunity to teach how to modulate moods or be respectful of others. Perhaps trouble offers a chance to bring out a quietly festering issue into the open.

When trouble comes knocking at my door, I will look for the opportunity hiding behind it.

August 8

*To help your children turn out well, spend
twice as much time with them and half
as much money.*

·~ H. Jackson Brown, Jr.

Many of us know people who grew up in the opposite situation: not enough attention from home and too much money. Most of us recognize that this combination often falls short on raising happy or healthy children.

Sure, our children ask for and want things, lots of things. But the way they really know they are worthwhile human beings is by how we parents want to hang out with them, by how much we know and enjoy them.

The next time I have a choice between spending time or money on my child, I will choose time.

August 9

Expect trouble as an inevitable part of life. . . .
Then repeat to yourself the most comforting
of all words, "This too shall pass."

~ Ann Landers

Even the best kids give parents some kind of trouble
once in a while. Perhaps your child is in a period
of having a bad attitude about something she has
always loved, or your child is struggling with a difficult class and not really handling it the way you
would like. Or it can be bigger trouble: your son was
caught doing drugs or drinking outside the school
dance. Some trouble requires parental action. There
are always resources available to help us figure this
out—friends, teachers, professionals.

Beyond doing what we need to do, it's time to
let go. Trouble, one way or another, shifts, changes,
and eventually moves on. And our children are so
much more than the trouble they create or get into.

Today I will be honest about my trouble, but keep it in
perspective.

August 10

What happens when we as parents don't ask for help from other adults, and other adults don't offer? Simple: our kids lose out.
·~ Kathleen Kimball-Baker

It has been well-documented that teens who have caring adults in their lives feel better about themselves and tend to make healthier choices for themselves. As parents, we want to do everything we can to encourage such relationships with adults we and our child trust.

It may be a special teacher, a coach, or program leader. If you're lucky, there's a grandparent or favorite aunt or uncle. Maybe it's one or more of their friends' parents. Know how important these relationships are for your child and nurture them. Invite them for dinner, encourage your teen to spend time with them, and above all, let these people know how much you appreciate what they bring to your teen's life.

Today I will encourage and appreciate a special adult in my child's life.

August 11

*Once adolescence begins, teenage boys go
to their room, close the door, turn on their
stereo, and come out four years later.*

— Dr. Anthony E. Wolf

This piece of information can go a long way toward
allaying fears about what is wrong with your son,
with you as a parent, with your family. The questions "Why doesn't he want to talk to me anymore?"
and "What is he doing in there?" seem to go hand-
in-hand. Knowledgeable people tell us that boys
need space and privacy—so much of what they are
going through is about their bodies and sexuality.

Knowing what is normal and what isn't can be
helpful. Knowing we are not alone is essential. Knowing they will emerge from time to time, and more so
as they mature, can help us to have patience with this
phase.

*If my child needs privacy, I can honor this need with-
out taking it personally.*

August 12

*Centering: that act which precedes all others
on the potter's wheel.*
— Mary Caroline Richards

Before any shape emerges from the clay that is spinning on a wheel, the wet, as yet shapeless clay must be smoothed and centered. Beautiful and useful shapes can then emerge.

As parents, this is an image to hold close to our hearts, whether we are being asked to shape a fair consequence, a balance between limitations and privileges, or a choice that is laden with ripple effects. If we first center ourselves, then our thinking and decision-making will be strong and sturdy, from the center out.

I will do one thing today to center myself before I make any decisions about my teen: meditate, walk, talk to a good friend, or say a prayer.

August 13

A child enters your home and for the next twenty years makes so much noise you can hardly stand it. The child departs, leaving the house so silent you think you are going mad.

· ~ John Andrew Holmes

The noise level (and perhaps the mess level) of living with adolescents requires two things: acceptance and negotiation. As parents with different interests in music and volume of all sorts, it requires a kind of openness and patience to live compatibly with teens. They're noisy; they're messy. On the bright side, they fill your house with an energy that can make you green with envy. It really is to be enjoyed and savored: remind yourself, daily if necessary, that you will miss all this full-of-life energy when it moves on.

Since we are training our children to live and work with others, sometimes negotiation is the lesson. There may be days when you are too tired for the noise; it is okay to set limits when you need to. And our teens need to learn how to help clean up the messes.

I will enjoy the clatter of my child today, and negotiate when and where I need to.

August 14

Love is what you've been through with somebody.

— James Thurber

In a family's life there are many ups and downs. On the down side there may be loss of family members, loss of pets, loss of innocence. Sickness of any sort pulls a family into turbulent waters. But there will also be the highs of successful moments and achievements by family members.

Sometimes we weather the bad times better than other times. Sometimes we hurt each other, and other times we comfort each other through the tough periods. But it is going through the hard times and coming out the other side, still together, that strengthens the bonds of love.

The love I have for my teen is made of all the experiences and years we've shared.

August 15

Disrespect is the weapon of the weak and a defense against one's own despised and unwanted feelings.

-- Alice Miller

Disrespectful talk or behavior from our children is always unsettling. It's good to remember that we ourselves can slip into being disrespectful: we are not immune to this, either. Although it's not something any of us want to encourage, it's helpful to look deeper. Disrespect is a weapon of the weak. So, why is our teen feeling weak? Why are we? Beneath the behavior, what are the negative feelings?

Beyond not allowing or encouraging disrespectful behavior from my teen, I can take time to wonder and ask about the feelings beneath the behavior.

August 16

Health is the condition of wisdom, and the sign is cheerfulness—an open and noble temper.

·- Ralph Waldo Emerson

I love the idea that health, wisdom, and cheerfulness go together. Often the impediments to cheerfulness are qualities like self-pity, resentment, and unexpressed anger. So perhaps a vital part of health and wisdom is moving through those dark, difficult feelings into the bright light of positive ones.

Whatever anger or resentment you might feel as a parent, there are ways to get through it. Often this means talking to a trusted person and receiving a dose of support and empathy. The important thing is not to wallow. Instead, work to move into a place of cheerful acceptance after wrestling with what you need to do to make this transformation.

I will do one thing today to move away from resentment or self-pity, and instead move toward health, wisdom, and cheerfulness.

August 17

The atmosphere parents wish to create when talking with children about birth and reproduction is a warm, honest, and reassuring one that tells children they are free to ask questions as often as they need to, and you will answer them as lovingly as you know how.

— Joanna Cole

All the experts tell me I should be talking to my children about drugs and sexuality. A long time ago I would have thought such conversations would come easily for me, not awkwardly like it was with my own mother. But I find these conversations very difficult at times. I'm surprised to find that I do feel nervous sometimes or at least self-conscious.

When dealing with hard topics, give yourself permission to be clumsy. Better to be clumsy than completely quiet on these important issues. I can attest that, at least with my older teenager, these conversations are becoming easier. But they wouldn't be if I hadn't pushed myself. It takes a dose of courage to approach these subjects, but it's important to do so.

Important conversations are not always easy to initiate, but they're worth the discomfort.

August 18

Remember, when they have a tantrum, don't have one of your own.

— Dr. Judith Kuriansky

As obvious and silly as it sounds, this sentiment holds a deep wisdom. A tantrum from a child of any age can so easily trigger the child within us. There's the child who starts yelling at his mother because he has no clean socks. There's the teenager who lets loose because there is no car available for her use. There's the tired teen who starts swearing because there are no sharp pencils in the house.

Some days it doesn't take much to set off these already edgy creatures. And if we, the parents, are vulnerable in any way—tired, rundown, disappointed— watch out. Our biggest challenge is to hold steady. We can firmly set guidelines on expected behavior without yelling or swearing. A parental temper tantrum never creates winning results. It only pulls us down into a muddy quagmire and often takes the focus away from where it really belongs.

I can stay strong when I need to and resist sliding down the tantrum hole—in this way I won't pollute the problem.

August 19

Faith is like radar that sees through the fog—the reality of things at a distance that the human eye cannot see.

·~ Corrie ten Boom

Most of us will go through a difficult time with our teenagers or, at the very least, experience a worry or two. When we are concerned about some aspects of our teenagers, we first need to figure out what action is required. Beyond that, we must dig deep and find faith in whatever form works for us.

Although we can't always see the outcome, it helps immensely to have faith that out there, beyond the range of our vision, lies a path we cannot yet see. We will find our way, and so will our teenagers.

I will let the radar of faith give me hope that my teen and I will find our way, even if it isn't clear yet.

August 20

There are high spots in all of our lives and most of them have come about through encouragement from someone else.

.~ George Matthew Adams

As parents we are in key positions to encourage our children in their talents and interests, and to encourage their friends as well. We can never gauge when our words, enthusiasm, or appreciation might make a difference for a child, but we can never go wrong by being generous. A compliment, a gesture, applause, all go a long way toward encouraging others. We shouldn't let shyness or self-consciousness stop us.

We are also modeling key aspects of mutual support when we encourage our friends, other family members, and other parents. People who do well almost always have a lot of people supporting them.

I will be generous with words of encouragement today— for my child and my friends.

August 21

*Since nothing we intend is ever faultless, and
nothing we attempt ever without error . . .
we are saved by forgiveness.*

~ David Augsburger

The need to forgive ourselves for not being perfect
parents comes often and is always humbling. Besides
the fact that teens are usually the first to point out
our shortcomings, most of us are also pretty hard on
ourselves. This arises from our genuine, deeply felt
desire to be good parents, perhaps specifically to do
a few things better than our own parents did.

Yet our own flaws can get in the way of our
parenting—our own distractions, misplaced pri-
orities, fears, self-consciousness, or sense of inade-
quacy. Being aware of when this interferes with our
relationships with our children is important. But even
more important is a moment of kindness toward ourselves, as we honestly admit our own imperfections.

*Today I will be aware of one flaw that affects who I am
as a parent, and I will ask to be willing to forgive myself
for this.*

August 22

*The most beautiful discovery true friends
make is that they can grow separately without growing apart.*

― Elisabeth Foley

We will watch our children go through many different stages with friendships. It is sometimes difficult
for them if a friend takes up a new sport or a new relationship. They can feel left out and as if the friendship is no longer there. As parents we often see the
bigger picture, and we can help balance out the extreme responses our kids go through from time to
time. They are just learning how to deal with hurt
feelings and disappointments in friendship.

Perhaps you have a friendship that has changed
over time due to various life circumstances. If you
still keep in touch in a new and slightly different
way, you can point this out to your child. Open and
accepting hearts can realize that friendships change,
and remain open to the connection the change
might bring. With a little effort friendships can still
thrive, even in the midst of change.

*I can nurture the idea that friendships will change but
can be kept alive in new ways.*

August 23

Trust your intuitive heart.

~ Richard Carlson

Your child seems quiet lately. Although she says she is fine, your heart tells you something else. You arrange a special dinner for her with her favorite older cousin, and she comes home and tells you how her friends have been mean to her. Her cousin helped her see what was going on and encouraged her to talk to you. If you hadn't listened to your heart, this down period may have gone on and on. After talking, you and she work out some solutions, and in the next few days her social life and her mood have brightened considerably.

Sometimes a child needs quiet time or family time but doesn't know it and can't quite ask for it. Sometimes a child is struggling with a class and needs extra homework help. An intuitive heart is a form of radar, a way of detecting what isn't yet visible. More than anything, it requires tuning in to your child and to your own listening frequency.

My intuitive heart is a huge asset in my life as a parent. I will honor it today.

August 24

*Empathy feels these thoughts; your hurt is
in my heart, your loss is in my prayers, your
sorrow is in my soul, and your tears are in
my eyes.*

— William A. Ward

Empathy is defined as the ability to share in another's emotions or feelings. Often this is what our children most need from us. Sometimes we must banish the reflexive impulse to fix things for our kids, and instead simply try to understand their feelings, especially the ones that are so painful to witness. It's a step we often forget to make or take time for.

If your teen is heartbroken, angry, disappointed, or feeling sad, your ability to empathize and to understand, quite simply, what he or she is feeling is the best way to make a connection. As a parent, this is often what you also need from your most supportive friends.

*Before any call to action, let me remember to empathize
with the raw feelings my teen is going through.*

August 25

Drugs and drinking are embedded in the fabric of the world of which our teenagers too are a part. . . . We cannot fully protect them from it. We can try, and our efforts can make a difference.

— Dr. Anthony E. Wolf

Embedded in this statement is the sad and alarming reality that our children are living in a culture in which alcohol and other drugs are readily available. In some peer groups it is more prevalent than in others, but even the most straitlaced of students will find themselves around it. One of the most important things we need to do is acknowledge this reality, not ignore it.

We can make a difference in our children's lives. We have some leverage in our hands. And hopefully, what we value and expect also matters to our kids. But we are not omnipresent enough to completely control our teens.

I will do one thing today to not ignore the availability of drinking and other drugs in the world my child lives in.

August 26

Since you are like no other being ever created since the beginning of time, you are incomparable.

— Brenda Ueland

Comparing oneself to others is always a slippery slope. It has a habit of making us feel superior or inferior in ways that are seldom authentically connected to who we really are. And as parents, the comparison trap can become complex. We compare ourselves as parents to other parents, we compare our children to other children. We watch or listen to our children compare themselves to others.

Hard as it is, the impulse to compare needs to be brought back to center. How we are doing as parents and how our children are doing has nothing to do with Johnny from next door. Each of us is an individual, with a unique style as a parent and human being. Our kids are also distinctive, each one requiring a slightly unique approach and touch.

Rather than compare, I will take a deep breath and clarify what I need today and what my unique child needs today.

August 27

*Love and time, those are the only two things
in all the world and all of life that cannot be
bought, but only spent.*

— Gary Jennings

Love and time—two of the most important gifts we
give to our children. Even teenagers need the affection and attention of their parents, and it's helpful
to create avenues to give it. Special dinners together
or road trips are wonderful and natural ways to just
be together.

Are there any activities you and your teen both
enjoy? Perhaps it's skiing together, or cooking together, or walking the dog. In the end, of all the
things we give our children, love and time will be
the most sustaining gifts and influences.

*Today I will remember to love my teenager by making
some time to be with her or him.*

August 28

*When you recover or discover something
that nourishes your soul and brings joy, care
enough about yourself to make room for it
in your life.*

— Dr. Jean Shinoda Bolen

Nourishing your soul, inviting joy into your life, and
caring about yourself are all values most of us believe in for ourselves and for our children. Yet we can
forget to make time for these values in the scramble
to pay our bills and keep track of our schedule and
our children's schedules. So when an activity or a
place beckons to us, lighting up a special place in our
hearts, it's time to reach out for it.

How will our children know how to care about
themselves if they don't see us model it? And joy is
a wonderful element to bring into family life. For
one couple a rekindled joy might be in ballroom
dancing; for one dad, it might be fishing; for another mom, it might be playing the flute in a neighborhood orchestra.

*Today I will care enough about myself to take time for
something I love to do.*

August 29

> *[Parents] are usually required to act on the spur of the moment—there is not time to go and consult the books and see what one ought to be doing.*
>
> — Sheila Kitzinger

No matter how well-prepared we think we might be, no matter how clear we want to be about certain lines, boundaries, or privileges, teens can always catch us off-guard and surprise us.

In these moments we do the best we can, scraping by on instinct and past experience. Some days we will do well and feel good about our response. On other days we'll think our spur-of-the-moment reaction was a mistake. This is part of parenthood: when a ballplayer gets a surprise ball hit in his direction, sometimes he'll catch it, and other times he'll miss.

I can forgive myself if a last-minute surprise request caught me off-guard. I can pat myself on the back if it didn't.

August 30

*We have only this moment, sparkling like a
star in our hand—and melting like a snow-
flake. Let us use it before it is too late.*
·- Marie Beynon Ray

The moment sparkles; it's a beautiful summer day
and instead of going back to work after your daughter's dental appointment, the two of you grab your
bikes and soak up the blazing sun and fresh air.
Years later she talks of that time as being a special
memory. Your son leans on the counter and starts
to talk about his girlfriend for the first time. You
sink into the nearest chair and delay your next task.

These are spontaneous decisions, decisions to
seize the moment. These are times when your child
is open to talking to you, open to playing with you,
open to being who he or she truly is with you.
They are rare and special moments, for so much of
your child's attention is far away from where you
are. I recently read of a father who lost his son. His
biggest regret? Missing such moments.

*Today I will seize the special moment with my child—
a moment to listen or to play.*

August 31

*I've seen some good examples of kids who
have been helped to know themselves and
then pursue activities that are fitting.*

·~ Dr. Mel Levine

There are numerous ways for a child or, for that matter, an adult to get to know himself or herself better. Some classes provide this opportunity through writing or other creative explorations. Another way is for teens of any age to write down their goals or interests.

It is always a positive thing for kids to do this, and the beginning of the school year is a particularly good time. Then we can help them pursue activities, explore their interests, or figure out the next step in meeting their goals. Interests and passions motivate people of all ages, and it's no different for our teens.

Today I will encourage my child to be aware of her or his goals, and then I will honor my child's interests in a concrete way.

September 1

Knowledge is power.

— Francis Bacon

Our children need information, especially about the temptations of their time—drugs, alcohol, sex. I recently heard a teenager say, "I had no idea what drinking straight shots could do to a person." We sometimes think our kids are exposed to so much that they know everything. But their information about the hard physical realities of sex, drugs, and alcohol is often patchy. We can help them by giving them information through talks, or by getting books for them, or hooking them up with experts in these areas.

The more knowledge and information our children have, the better equipped they are for navigating their world.

Where might my teen need more basic information? I will list possibilities and come up with a way to empower her or him with information.

September 2

*A great man always considers the timing
before he acts.*

~ Chinese proverb

My daughter has a tendency to overbook herself.
This became clear to me one morning at 6:00 when
I was waking her after a late night of studying on
her part. I wanted to talk about it right then and
there, but I literally bit my tongue.

Because I've gone down that road before, I know
that trying to talk to her when she's just woken up
is a conversation that goes nowhere or, more accurately, spins off in a negative and fruitless direction.
But if I wait until later, until what I've come to call
a "talkable moment" arises, she might actually hear
me. Such a moment requires a sense of calm on
both of our parts and some time to talk, without
the added pressure of being in a hurry.

*If I want to be heard, I need to choose a moment when
my child feels open to a conversation.*

September 3

An empty sort of mind is valuable for find-ing pearls and tails and things because it can see what's in front of it. An overstuffed mind is unable to.

- Benjamin Hoff

In the world of parenting, "finding pearls and tails" might mean something along the lines of seeing your child's strengths clearly, or figuring out what your child needs today. It might mean knowing you just need to sit with your child for a while today. It might mean knowing you need time alone or with a good friend to rejuvenate yourself.

It helps us as human beings and parents to clear our minds. The purpose is to clarify our vision, our mind's eye. On the other side of muddled thinking is the opportunity for clarity.

Today I will think of a way to clear myself of cluttered thinking and do it.

September 4

And whether or not it is clear to you, no
doubt the universe is unfolding as it should.
— Max Ehrmann

It can be difficult to believe that the universe is unfolding as it should in our own lives, and that difficulty can multiply when we observe our children going through the normal ups and downs of adolescence. What can seem to be a crisis or even just a mistake in the moment can take on the light of a beneficial learning experience with a little distance.

If we as parents trust in the inherent goodness of the universe, in this gentle and positive unfolding, we help plant a seed of faith and hope in our children. If we want them to see what's right in this world rather than what is wrong, it needs to start with us.

Today I will trust that all in my teen's and my universe
is unfolding just as it should be.

September 5

*Lectures do very little. . . . it makes us feel
better. We should not delude ourselves as
to who it is that benefits from our lectures.*
— Dr. Anthony E. Wolf

We have all fallen into the lecture trap. Who doesn't
like the idea that simply stating our hard-earned
pearls of wisdom and our clear expectations will
make teens do what we want them to do? Most of
us are attached to the idea that what we say has an
impact, but we forget the difference between lecture
and dialogue.

When we lecture others, the listener goes to
sleep. If it's not a dialogue, it's not going to work.
We may please ourselves, we may immerse ourselves
in the glorious illusion that simply saying what we
want will make it happen. But what we're really doing
is creating barriers rather than connections.

*For today I will write my lecture down or tell it to a
friend instead of delivering it to my teen.*

September 6

. . . remind me that I must try to be alone . . .
for part of each day, even for an hour or a few
minutes in order to keep my core, my center,
my island-quality.

— Anne Morrow Lindbergh

In the course of life's business, this is easy to forget. We all need this reminder: to preserve a few moments, at least, in each day to keep our central core lit and burning. For me, if I have a cup of coffee alone in the morning, I am a much better human being as I wake my family and get the ball rolling for the day. It helps clear my brain and open my heart to the day.

There are numerous ways parents can center themselves. You might read for a few minutes every day, or take regular evening walks around the block. One friend takes time between the office and home to exercise so that when she returns home she can fully be there with and for her teenagers. Another friend loves music—and she knows that if she makes time to enjoy it she is a much happier mom.

Today I will remember to take a few moments for myself.

September 7

Kids want to be loved. They want and need to know their specialness.

·– Patty Wetterling

In the face of sullen, withdrawn teenagers or crabby, overbusy ones, it's easy to feel as if they don't want your love. This need for affection can be especially hard to see when it seems buried under a mountain of demands—school papers that must be signed and returned, forms for athletic clothes that need to be ordered, and, of course, checks that must be written.

No matter what our teens' moods or activity levels may be, and no matter how demanding they are, we need to remember that they all want and need to be loved. Find a way to let them know what is special and unique about them every day: Laugh at his joke, admire the earrings she just put on, point out when he or she has done a good job in any area.

As special as I know my child to be, I will remember today to express that uniqueness, to celebrate some part of her or him.

September 8

A pat on the back, though only a few vertebrae removed from a kick in the pants, is miles ahead in results.

— Bennett Cerf

I like to think that every positive comment given to a child is a golden thread that connects child to parent—not in a binding or constrictive way, but in a caring and healing way. People of all ages respond better to praise than to criticism. And we need to keep remembering that with our children.

If teens feel like it's possible and easy to please you, they will. If they feel you are impossible to please, they may well quit trying. It's a simple thing to tell your child you noticed his good sportsmanship at the track meet, his kindness to his sister, his efforts at practicing or studying, his being more willing than usual to get out of bed in the morning. Even small positive steps, if given recognition, will grow more quickly.

I will pay attention today to something positive my child has done and I will let her know I noticed.

September 9

You and your child are both souls; you are
both embarked on the journey of soul-making.
  .~ Deepak Chopra

Parent and child help shape each other. What we
share is a home and a journey through this stage of
life together. Both parent and child are involved in
soul making, which is really the process of becoming more spiritually alive and knowing who we are
and what we are here on this planet for.

Although teens are in the early stages of life, we
can respect their soul journeys as we also respect
our own.

As a parent, I need to respect that my teen has her or his
own soul journey, a unique path.

September 10

*Perhaps the greatest social service that can
be rendered by anybody to the country and
to mankind is to bring up a family.*

— George Bernard Shaw

Performance reviews, promotions, and pay raises
don't exist in the world of parenting, yet parenting
truly is one of the areas in which we will make our
most important contributions and leave our most
enduring legacies. I recently read an article about
a very accomplished man—financially, career-wise,
politically—whose child had committed suicide. He
said that in that moment, all his accomplishments
felt like nothing. His biggest regret was not having
paid enough attention to his son.

Although many parents try to balance a career
life and a home life, it is easy to shortchange our
children. It is tempting to get swept up in the world
of pay raises and to pay less attention to the daily
regimen of parenting. Quite simply it all comes down
to paying attention, taking time to talk with your
child, to check in with your child, to reinforce the
values you want your child to have.

*Being a parent is my most important job. I will give it
the attention and intention it deserves.*

September 11

*An adventure is only an inconvenience
rightly considered. An inconvenience is only
an adventure wrongly considered.*

— G. K. Chesterton

Being a parent is one of the ultimate adventures;
along the way are many smaller adventures that disguise themselves as inconveniences. There is little
about parenting that is convenient. It is full of surprises, unexpected challenges, and reversals.

Rather than feeling weighted down by every small
inconvenience, we can begin to look for the adventures disguised within them. A teen who flattens a
tire on the family car learns an important lesson about
how to repair it and ask for help. A child who breaks
her leg salvages the weeks spent in a cast by learning
a new piece on the piano. Delivering your son to and
from school adds an hour to your day, but you get a
chance to chat with his teachers during this time.

*When I feel ruffled by inconvenience I can look for the
adventurous edge it might hold.*

September 12

Fear wants us to act too soon. But patience,
hard as it is, helps us outlast our preconceptions.
.~ Mark Nepo

When children get in trouble, and most of them do at least once in a while, it can set off our parental fears. We jump quickly to worst-case scenarios, and, of course, we fear that we haven't been good enough parents. Fear can make us react in the heat of the moment, impulsively and not from the best part of ourselves.

Patience that is born of looking clearly and fully at a picture, not denying it, is the kind of patience that nourishes our role as parents. Sometimes a situation requires further conversation, help from an outside source, time to see more clearly. Time widens the scope of our lens.

Today I will nurture a clear-eyed patience as I look at and love my teen.

September 13

*Your family and your love must be cultivated
like a garden. Time, effort, and imagination
must be summoned constantly to keep [any
relationship] flourishing and growing.*

— Jim Rohn

A neglected child is a lonely one. And lonely children tend to get into more trouble than other kids. But that isn't the only reason we parents want to tend to the garden of raising children. It's also because this garden, tended, bears beautiful and useful fruit. Children who are honored by their parents' time and efforts, who are beneficiaries of their parents' imaginations, flourish in ways that are fun and rewarding to be a part of.

It is the ongoing need for nurturing that can sometimes wear us out or catch us off-guard. But we can always find a way to renew ourselves and get back on track. Back to the garden, back to paying attention, back to the conscious effort to grow loving children.

*I will look around today and see where my child might
need some time, effort, or imagination from me.*

September 14

Like a welcome summer rain, humor may suddenly cleanse and cool the earth, the air and you.

~ Langston Hughes

Is there someone in your family who is good at lightening things up? Especially good at seeing the humor in life? This is a real gift, and one that should be honored and given space. Humor can give a fresh perspective to an ordinary day or a challenging situation.

Humor expresses itself in many ways. Sometimes it's the sharing of wacky jokes, or laughing together at the antics of the family pet, or sharing a humorous story about an extended family member. Humor in a family helps lighten everyone's mood and creates a connection that is laced with a loving, light touch.

Today I will remember to laugh with my family.

September 15

In just about every way imaginable [teens are] inhabiting bodies that become more unfamiliar with each passing day. And to make matters worse, young teens often feel like they're on stage.

~ Susan Panzarine

We cannot underestimate how bewildering it is for our teens to be going through so many physical changes, and to be surrounded by others going through so many changes. None of it is hidden. Body shapes and sizes are often a subject of conversation, even intense scrutiny. Everybody sees, everybody notices. And yet at the same time, it's an intensely personal journey.

As awkward as it can be, gently entering into conversations about body issues whenever you find an opening is a good thing. They need answers to their questions, along with concrete things like deodorant, jock straps, or bras. Do what you can to make the conversations open, even if you do hear the proverbial embarrassed, "Oh, Mom!" or "Dad, I already know everything."

I will remember today that my teen needs information about her or his body and encouragement to ask me questions directly.

September 16

You may strive to be like them, but seek not to make them like you, for life goes not backward nor tarries with yesterday.

         – Kahlil Gibran

My son has a way of processing music at the piano that is very different from mine. If I'm trying to help him and I push him to look at the music the way I do, it's guaranteed we'll both become irritated. My daughter can juggle many more activities than I ever could at her age, and I sometimes try to instill my sense of caution in her. She doesn't appreciate this and lets me know.

In both instances I am trying to impose my way upon them as if it was the "better" way, which is always a recipe for frustration. And the potential for such frustration is huge and presents itself daily. Yet, if I can step back and take a deep breath, I may well end up admiring them for their own ways of coping. Or at the very least, I can accept that my teens have their own ways.

Today I will accept and honor the many ways my teen differs from me.

September 17

Of course some behavior is dangerous to the child and to others. Express your concern with the behavior. Do not attack the child.

~ William Martin

There is a difference between saying, "You're so careless," and, "That was a careless thing to do. You can do better than that." We are going to run into behaviors we don't like, as well as behaviors we know aren't healthy. So, the question is, how do we deal with this?

Expressing concern is always a loving thing to do, even if it isn't received as such. Expressing concern holds up the mirror to our child; it raises, rather than ignores, an issue. Concern also lets them know you care and opens the door for consequences or further discussion. This approach will always be more fruitful than judging or attacking who they are.

If I feel an impulse to judge my child today, I will reframe my thinking and focus on my concerns.

September 18

Friendship makes the world go around.
— Mary Simons

For many of us parents it is our friends who help us out when we're in need and who brighten and light up our days. Friendship is important to our teens as well. As parents, we always want to encourage the friendships that bring kindness and positive energy into our teens' lives. Friendships make everything more fun, are often integral to the learning process, and help teens navigate the rough waters around them.

If your teen has friendships that concern you, one way to deal with that is to encourage the friendships that seem more positive. If you can see that your teen has friendships that are good for her or him, then you need to remember how lucky you are. For while adults tend to provide the safe harbor for them, it's their friends who are their true traveling companions.

Today I will notice where my teen has strong healthy friendships, or where he or she may need some encouragement in the friendship arena.

September 19

*When one tugs at a single thing in nature, he
finds it attached to the rest of the world.*

~ John Muir

All of nature is interconnected. And as family
members, as members of a school community, a
neighborhood community, and any other community we belong to, we are as connected to each other
as plants are to the earth. The more our children
see and feel these connections, the more they see
that their choices and actions matter.

The neighbor who is genuinely interested in your
teen, who teaches him to garden or asks her to help
with a block party, is a real asset for your teen and
thus for you, the parent, as well. The five-year-old
up the street who adores your teenager is an asset
too—a source of love for your teen and someone
your teen can inspire and model good behavior for.
As parents, the more we encourage, pay attention
to, and enable these interconnections for our teens,
the more they know they matter—to a whole web
of people.

*Today I will appreciate all the people who help "watch
out" for the best interests of my child.*

September 20

One of the secrets of a happy life is continu-
ous small treats.

— Iris Murdoch

When my children were young, we used to go to the corner store, where I would treat myself to my favorite coffee drink and they would each buy a small treat. Even on the days when someone was crabby, overtired, or just getting over being sick, this simple ritual always brightened and lightened our hearts.

The ability to appreciate and celebrate simple treats is a huge part of feeling content or happy. Notice it in your child: does she brighten up when she finds her favorite treat in the freezer? When her best friend walks in the door? Notice it in yourself: Do flowers make your day special? Being grateful for the small treats in life makes for happy minds, bodies, and spirits.

Today I will give myself a small treat and feel grateful for it.

September 21

To listen is an effort, and just to hear is no merit. A duck hears also.

‑ Igor Stravinsky

Listening requires more than one ear, more than half of one's mind on the conversation. It requires being fully present in the moment and not worrying about the past or planning the future. Sometimes true listening means sensing what is not being said but is being expressed through body language or mood.

A person who is not listened to, whether adult or teen, begins to feel unimportant and invisible. Listening to each other is a simple gift, but requires the effort of focus and emotional presence. It is an integral part of any true conversation.

Today I will remember to be present and really listen to what my child says with words and expressions.

September 22

*. . . if you praise your child . . . He will smile
on the inside. She will believe she can do other
things, too.*

— Esther Davis-Thompson

At the end of the day or week, do you sometimes
realize how the quiet thoughts about how well your
teen did something never made it past your lips?
Such positive thoughts can flicker across the brain
and then get quickly lost in the busyness and inter-
ruptions of our lives.

Just as we respond to praise, so do our teens. If
there is something praiseworthy you noticed, write
about it in a note to your child. Or call her or him
on the phone during a break at work. Or vow to
take time today to praise what you have noticed
your teen doing. Positive comments that are shared
and expressed help our teens keep building who they
are in an upbeat and uplifting way.

*Today I will take time to praise my teen for one specific
thing I admire.*

September 23

There are times in life when one does the right thing.

·- Ellen Bass

Most of us have moments where we know we did the right thing. Perhaps you offered a word of empathy at a vulnerable moment for your child and it was obviously appreciated. Perhaps a teenage son thanked his mom for making him practice the guitar because he has finally become skilled enough to play in a band. Perhaps a mother redirected her daughter's interest away from worrisome friends by enrolling her in dance classes; they both discovered her daughter loves dance.

If we scan over our recent parenting experiences these moments are often there, quietly waiting to be noticed. Sometimes we skip over them, in a hurry to get onto the next one. But these moments should be cherished; they almost always evoke a feeling of tenderness in us. We are our children's parents, and we do get it right sometimes.

Today I will quietly celebrate one thing I have done right with or for my teen recently.

September 24

*A book should serve as the ax for the frozen
sea within us.*

— Franz Kafka

Books often open doors to new insights, or deepen existing insights. Books can be conveyors of useful and vital information for the situations life throws at us. Books placed in the hands of teens at strategic moments are priceless.

Although never a complete replacement for discussion or conversation, books can be incredibly helpful tools. Many parents have found the right book at the right time to be a godsend. If our children are struggling with body image or with friendships or in choosing a college, there may well be a book that will be useful. It's always helpful to know others struggle with the same issues.

Today I will look for a book or magazine article that might be useful for my teen.

September 25

Consistency is really a part of order, and as such helps to establish boundaries and limitations that provide the child with a sense of security.

－ Dr. Rudolph Dreikurs

Children of all ages need to feel a sense of order in their lives. A gathering together at mealtime, whenever possible, is one way to build in them this kind of order. Expectations about school and a designated place to do homework also help establish a sense of order. Providing outlets for their activities or developing their skills are other ways to provide order. A teen who has basketball practice every day and a drum lesson once a week is a teen who has order in her or his life.

Without going overboard with rules, regulations, or regimentation, we can provide a steady beat for our children. We need to be consistent, like the background drummer in a band. If he or she is erratic, everybody's rhythm is thrown off. A sense of security (or song) disintegrates quickly.

Where it's important, I will be consistent regarding my teen's schedule, need for help, or consequences.

September 26

Those who have suffered understand suffering and therefore extend their hand.

·– Patti Smith

As parents, we all are in need of support from time to time. Isn't it interesting that it's easiest to reach out to those who you know have also gone through hard times. Experience most often gives birth to empathy and the knowledge that what a person really needs in a hard moment is acceptance, understanding, a hand to hold.

So, if you are worried about your daughter who got caught drinking again, or if your child won't talk to you anymore, or your child keeps getting sick, reach out. There is someone around you who has struggled and is ready to extend his or her hand.

When I need to, I can reach out and find understanding. This is also how I learn the essence of being able to support other parents in their time of need.

September 27

It is better to light one candle than curse the darkness.

.- Christopher Society Motto

When you're feeling down and out, do one positive thing. When darkness seems to surround you, move toward that tiny pinprick of existing light. Light a candle and in doing so, look around and see your life in a new and brighter way.

If you have a child who struggles with chemical dependency or depression, make a phone call or go to a meeting. Remind yourself that you are nowhere near alone in the world with this problem. If you are struggling with making a decision about your child or yourself, take a long clarifying walk and be grateful that you can. Almost any darkness can be lit up, if you only reach toward the light.

I will light a candle today by reaching beyond the darkness in my life.

September 28

Children have more need of models than of critics.

 ·~ Joseph Joubert

Nothing sets a teen on edge more quickly than criticism. And if most of us are honest, we remember all too vividly the times we were criticized when we were younger. So much of the teen years is about coming of age, emerging, trying things on, trying to figure out who and what they are. Gentle acceptance will create a much stronger bond than harsh criticism.

Model the qualities you want to teach and this will be far more powerful than any criticism.

Today I will turn any criticism I feel toward my teen into an understanding that how I act—not what I say—matters the most.

September 29

*One ought, every day at least, to hear a little
song, read a good poem, see a fine picture
and, if it were possible, to speak a few reasonable words.*

~ Johann von Goethe

Part of our job as parents is to expose our children to
the joys of music, the open windows of reading books
and poems, the beauty that exists in this world, and
the joy of connecting with others. It sounds like a
long list but it really is doable.

Do you have poems and good books around the
house? Do you enjoy reading them yourself? How
about letting your child tape a favorite poem to the
kitchen cupboard for both of you to enjoy? When
was the last time your teen felt inspired enough to
sing or recite a favorite song to you? Sharing a love of
music or learning is a really fun part of parenting.

*Today I will look for an opportunity to share my favor-
ite music, or another art form I enjoy, with my teen.*

September 30

Trust yourself. You know more than you think you do.

— Dr. Benjamin Spock

Although we all have our blind spots, we also intuitively know our children in a way that no one else does. Sometimes, what we most need to do is rely on that knowledge and trust what we are feeling inside our bodies.

If something feels wrong and tugs at our hearts, we really need to pay attention to that. If we sense our child needs more support in some area, we can trust that knowledge and act on it. The important thing is to listen to ourselves, to trust ourselves, and to honor how much we know our teenager.

Today I will take some time to reflect and see if there's something I am feeling about my teen that I need to trust more fully.

October 1

Where there is not discernment, the be-
havior even of the purest soul may in effect
amount to coarseness.

.-- Henry David Thoreau

Your teenager comes home with a far lower grade
than usual. Your child's teacher calls and is concerned about something that came up in class.
Another parent in the neighborhood makes a comment about your child. How do you decide how big
these problems are, or what they mean, or what response is best?

This question is huge and will come up over and
over again on the long and winding road of parenting teens. Discernment is the challenge here, and any
tools that help us are to be used. This might include
writing in a journal for clarity, practicing meditation,
or talking to good and trusted friends, teachers, or
a therapist. Teenage behavior that happens once in a
while is usually less serious than behavior that looks
like it's developing into a pattern.

Rather than reacting blindly to a problem or brushing it
aside, I will choose one or more ways to really consider
what is going on with my teen and to discern what I
need to do.

October 2

*Research shows that young people who have
a healthy connection to a congregation are less
likely to try risky behaviors and more likely
to make choices that help them succeed. . . .*
~ Kathleen Kimball-Baker

Being part of a faith community can be a real asset
for our children. It can provide another group of
caring kids and adults in their lives. Often religious
youth groups offer a forum for teens to look at their
values in a constructive, friendly environment. Even
if being part of an established faith doesn't work
for everyone in your family, there are other ways to
provide this experience for your child. For example,
some teens join a youth group at a friend's place of
worship.

If you are part of a faith community, plug your
child in from the earliest age possible. As a source of
support and personal reflection, such a community
can provide real comfort through the teen years.

*I will honor a spiritual connection in the life of my teen
by helping to make it possible and encouraging it.*

October 3

Luck is a matter of preparation meeting opportunity.

— Oprah Winfrey

Teens living with us are absorbing life lessons about many things: about moral values, about how we treat other human beings, about survival, about luck. Often luck is seen as something some people have and others don't. But we can begin to teach our teens about how hard work, linked to an opportunity, can look and feel like luck.

A teenage boy who thought he had no chance of making the varsity track team decides to commit himself to the running program as if he were. His time improves and two people on varsity are seriously injured. A place opens up on the team, and because of his hard work he is chosen to fill in for one of the injured team members. Luck? In a way. But it's mostly hard work and an unexpected door opening. It's a lesson most of us need to keep relearning.

Today I can pass on to my teenager the importance of discipline and preparation by encouraging her or him and by modeling both in my own life.

October 4

After a good dinner one can forgive anybody,
even one's own relations.

— Oscar Wilde

There's something tried and true about gathering
together around food. In today's world, with adults'
and kids' lives seemingly busier than ever before,
most of us have learned to be flexible about dinners. Rare are the days of my childhood when we
all gathered like clockwork every night at 6:00.

My own compromise is that Sunday nights are
a family feast. For a while I called it mandatory, but
now everyone just asks early in the day what we are
having. They look forward to it. It's usually the best
and most complete meal prepared in the course of
a week. If we eat together during the week, that's a
bonus. But Sunday nights have become a meal we
all look forward to. Even simple conversation at this
meal connects us.

Take time to plan a family meal. Enlist ideas for the
menu or conversation from your kids.

October 5

Comfort me when I fail.
— Search Institute survey respondent

A teenager might feel more comfortable writing this need than speaking it, but it's a need we would do well to remember. Part of our job as parents is to let teens spread their wings and try new things. Then we can welcome them back into the nest to strengthen themselves before the next flying lesson.

Sometimes our children just need to be comforted: she lost the class election; he injured himself and can't compete for three weeks; she didn't get into her first choice of college; he wasn't called back for auditions. In all these situations the comfort of empathy and a warm and accepting space at home helps enormously. Comfort at this time is the building ground for courage in the future.

When my teen is feeling down and out, what she needs from me more than anything is a moment of comfort and acceptance.

October 6

Especially with our first child, we tend to take too much responsibility—both credit and blame—for everything. The more we want to be good parents, the more we tend to see ourselves as making or breaking our children.

    ·– Polly Berrien Berends

When our children make mistakes—and they all do—most of us are quick to feel at fault. What did I say or do wrong, we ask ourselves. What could I or should I have done to prevent this? Why didn't I see this coming?

Our children come into this world as individuals, with their own wired-in challenges and weaknesses. We cannot save them from their own learning experiences, their own ups and downs. This is part of the human condition. We didn't cause their troubles and we can't cure them. We can only love them through their unique journeys.

Today I will remember that blaming myself is not where the truth lies. It lies in loving my child and myself fully, as best I can.

October 7

*It is very important for parents to under-
stand that adolescence does have an end, that
teenagers do change . . . and for the better.*
                                    ~ Dr. Anthony E. Wolf

Adolescence, at its simplest, is part of a much longer journey. In this phase, teens pull away from us
to create a sense of who they are individually. As
they try on who they are and begin to figure it out,
many of them relax and become quite interesting
and fascinating human beings. We get glimpses of
this in adolescence.

While they go through this process of self-
discovery, enjoy the glimpses and cherish the journey.
When it passes there will be aspects you will miss.
Such pure raw energy, such fun! There are great
clothes in my closet I never would have picked out
without my teen's insistence. There's music in our
collection we would have missed without the encouragement of our teens. This is just a small sampling of
how teens can enrich and nourish our lives.

*I will notice today at least one concrete way my life is
enriched by my teenager.*

October 8

Lift my head, help me up, / I am bruised,
bone and flesh; . . . .

— Hilda Doolittle

Whether it's a spouse, partner, relative, or friend, we all need others to help lift us up. A word of encouragement or empathy makes the world a less lonely place. Sometimes parenting can feel particularly lonely, and in those moments it's best to seek someone out, to know for a moment that two are better than one. Often we take turns being strong or being the one in need.

As we lean on other adults in our lives, our children absorb the knowledge that two are better than one. They will begin to mirror it in their own friendships. It is a gratifying thing to see your child hold a friend up or be supported through a difficult time by a friend. Ultimately, you and your children provide this kind of mutual support for each other, for the rest of your lives.

I will thank someone special for holding me up today.

October 9

*This kitchen table is my outpost, my place
to wait and worry. . . . I won't feel right till
she's home.*

·– Karen Loeb

Waiting and worrying are part of the parenting experience. As much as we can tell ourselves it does no good to worry, a certain amount of it is very human. The early weeks and months when a teen begins driving are usually particularly worrisome, with no shortage of potential fears on our part.

Most of us have our own "worrying command posts." It may be the kitchen table or it may be our bed. My dad used to wait up for me on our front porch when I rolled in late. Seeing him there set my heart racing. Only years later could I comprehend his sense of worry, of being on duty, of waiting, and his immense sense of relief when I arrived home, safe.

Today I will remember I am not alone when I wait and worry—I am part of a legacy and community of parenthood.

October 10

Happiness requires action.

— Jennifer James

Although happiness can seem like a fleeting emotion, there are daily choices we make about striving for and building happiness into our lives. As parents, this striving for happiness is an important quality to model. Instead of staying in jobs or relationships that bring us down, we can seek opportunities and experiences that are more positive or fit us better. If we are getting burned out at work, there are choices we must make to take care of ourselves, to feed a happier part of our lives.

It's important to transform into positive action our own tendency to whine or wallow and to strive for happiness in our daily lives. If we model positive action, we pass on the knowledge to our kids that they can always make choices in the direction of happiness. Taking action is much more fruitful than complaining.

Instead of whining I will choose to move toward happiness. My teen is learning by watching me.

October 11

Parents . . . are the "encouragers."
— Doris Bodmer

Our children are almost always stretching themselves—academically, athletically, socially. No matter what level they study or play at, you can bet they are often reaching and stretching beyond their comfort zone. That's what the teen and preteen years are all about—in fact, it may be what life—a growing life—is all about.

As parents, we get to help encourage our teens. *En*-courage them, literally helping them have courage. Offering positive comments, believing in them, and letting them know when they are doing well all help instill in them the courage to keep going. What helps you keep going? Take time to give teens the same kind of comfort and encouragement.

I will give my child one concrete positive comment today, to help en-courage him on his way.

October 12

Every man who knows how to read has it in his power to magnify himself, to multiply the ways in which he exists, to make his life full, significant and interesting.

– Aldous Huxley

The ability to read, study, and learn is a real and tangible asset for our children to have. Not only does learning give them a sense of competence, but it also opens up to them many worlds within our world. It helps them realize what a fascinating and amazing place is this country, this planet, and this universe.

If you have a reluctant reader, find books or magazines that speak to her or his interests. This is an excellent way to "hook" readers. If your child loves to read, keep making books available to her. It is also fun and rewarding when you can begin to share books with your teen and talk about books together.

There is a book out there waiting to connect me with my child—I will find it soon.

October 13

*Pain is important: how we evade it, how
we succumb to it, how we deal with it, how
we transcend it.*

.~ Audre Lorde

A lot of who we really are comes out of how we deal with obstacles and challenges. When all is going well it is easier to be a generous, strong, and principled person. It is much harder to nurture these qualities in times of loss.

Often we admire people who come through hard times gracefully. These are our models. As parents and as human beings, this is what we want to strive for: wrestling with our pain honestly and gracefully, and hopefully transcending it one day.

Whether my pain is internal or about my child, I can face it gracefully.

October 14

Control is not the key. Connection is. If we
have a connection with our kids, then we can
help them learn from their mistakes.

 — Dr. David Walsh

A basically caring, affectionate climate in a home
helps engender a sense of connection. Shared activities, in and out of the home, also help feed the connection that seems to slip away so easily. Helping
your child with homework or taking him shopping
for what he needs also helps.

When you find yourself frustrated and trying to
exert control, it might be helpful to back off. Think
of one genuine way to connect, one activity or one
thing about him that you really admire. Use it for
all it's worth. A child who is slipping in some way
needs desperately to know that his parents care.

I will remember today that I can help my child learn
from his mistakes if he knows that I am on his side.

October 15

*There are so many paradoxes in parenting
that it is difficult to find balance.*

~ William Martin

It is a truth about parenting that the experience is both intensely sweet and bitter. It is true that our children can bring us moments of exquisite joy and pride and then, almost simultaneously, drag us into the depths of anxiety or disappointment.

An emotional seesaw would be a good way to describe the experience. The challenge is for us to accept such a wide range of feelings, to honor all ends of the spectrum, and to find a way to be balanced in the process. It reminds me of the Zen meditation that advises us to watch our thoughts and not become too attached to any of them.

Today I will concentrate on keeping a sense of personal centeredness or balance as I experience the emotional ups and downs of being a parent.

October 16

The best things you can give children, next to good habits, are good memories.

— Sydney J. Harris

Most of us want to teach our teens good habits: some kind of work ethic, healthy eating habits, good manners. But we also want to be conscious of creating good memories for our teens. We can make sure that what we do together is fun and enjoyable. Is there a special restaurant you all enjoy going to together? Is there an annual trip you share fond memories of? Is there an activity you enjoy doing with each other?

If you have some shared memory-making already in place, make the most of it. If not, it might be good to look around and see where you might incorporate special activities into your family life.

One can't really plan a good memory, but as the parent I can make sure I help create shared times of fun and fondness.

October 17

Enthusiasm is the greatest asset in the world.
It beats money, power and influence.

— Henry Chester

A key to being a parent is noticing what your child is naturally enthusiastic about and then capitalizing on that. All children have passions, and if you can recognize them and help provide opportunities for developing those passions, then you are doing what you can to feed their enthusiasm.

Being able to practice or exercise what it is that makes them enthusiastic is truly an asset. Such passions give people of all ages energy, clarity, and focus. Energy and clarity and focus—these are truly gifts.

I will look today for where and how I am nurturing my child's enthusiasm.

October 18

We must all take the time to be silent and to contemplate. . . . It . . . gives you a clean and pure heart.

.- Mother Teresa

A parent's heart is easily cluttered. First, with the day-to-day business of living. Next, with all the emotional trappings of guilt, or unclear or unfair expectations, and finally with the unconscious imposition of our own childhoods upon who we are as parents.

To parent with a clear heart requires daily cleansing. Silence and contemplation, even in simple ways, can help clear us. Working on a crossword puzzle or reading a good book can help clear our thinking. Exercise or gardening are also helpful at times.

Today I will create enough space for a few moments of silence; with cleansed heart I am a better and more loving parent.

October 19

The first step in solving a problem is to tell someone about it.

.~ John Peter Flynn

Although we live in a culture that prizes and elevates perfection, no one's life is perfect. And it is in talking about the imperfections that we are vulnerable enough to really need, connect with, and appreciate each other. When we become brave enough to talk with our teenager, a professional, or a friend about a problem we are having, we discover we are not alone in having the problem or in figuring out what to do next.

This is an excellent coping skill to model and pass on to our children. When our teens encounter problems and if they have a trusted friend or professional to talk to, they will work their way through it with much more success and clarity. Teens will pick this up from what you model and what you give them permission to do.

Is there something I need to talk over with a trusted person today, or do I need to gently suggest my teen do the same?

October 20

. . . [G]rant me the . . . courage to change the
things I can, . . .

⸱- The Serenity Prayer

There are times in your life as a parent when you
will have to gird yourself and do the difficult thing.
Some parents will need to put their children into
treatment when alcohol or other drug usage is
clearly damaging their lives. Some parents will
need to choose a different school for a child based
on special needs. From time to time we all have to
get up our courage and talk straight about a difficult issue; there are many that will come up in the
course of living a life and raising children.

Whatever the source of our spiritual beliefs or
sustenance, we will need to ask for courage from this
source. Within each of us is a deep pool of courage
waiting for us to tap into it.

When and where I need courage, I can find it within.

October 21

If you want others to be happy, practice com-
passion. If you want to be happy, practice
compassion.

— The Dalai Lama

A teenage girl's unhappiness shows itself one morning through loud complaints and fuming: under-
neath the unpleasant behavior is the struggle to like
how she looks and feels in her clothes. A teen boy
comes home from school, crabby, having skipped
his sports practice. Both are struggling. As we deal
with the behavior, we parents need to be compassionate about what is rumbling around inside these
teens. They are often struggling with body image,
friend dilemmas, attention (or lack thereof) from
their crushes, feeling left out at school, or a host of
other possible issues.

Since all of these issues are not complete strang-
ers to us as adults, a compassionate awareness is
often within our reach. Heartfelt empathy and support, combined with working on behaviors, is an effective and positive way to connect with our teens'
world. This same compassion can also shine the light
of kindness into our own lives.

If I want my child or myself to feel happier, the first step
is compassion.

October 22

No matter how many communes anybody invents, the family always creeps back.

⁓ Margaret Mead

In her studies as an anthropologist Margaret Mead observed families in many parts of the world. This insight of hers speaks to the core human need we have for the family. It is parents and siblings living together that provides a sense of security and comfort for all, and especially so for a teen.

As much as your teen may have one foot out the door, as much as your daughter wants to shut you out, and as much as your son wishes he was at somebody else's house, they still need their own sense of family. Every young person needs strong family support in order to strive and thrive.

I will do one thing today that honors family support for my teen, even something as simple as having a meal together.

October 23

Life is an adventure in forgiveness.
— Norman Cousins

Family life can be the mountain made of mistakes and misunderstandings, the coming together of human flaws. Whatever each family member's flaws might be, it's a safe bet you've hurt one another through those flaws, often without ever intending to.

Thus there is the ongoing need we parents have for forgiveness. Perhaps we need to forgive a child for having hurt us in the process of their acting out or making a choice we disagreed with. Perhaps we ourselves need to be forgiven for unfairly judging our child based on a past experience. Forgiveness, although initially difficult, can help us move forward into healing and healthier moments.

Wherever I feel stuck in anger or disappointment, I can take comfort in forgiveness.

October 24

[Some children] question every lesson. . . . We love them so much, but they keep us perched on the edge of reason. . . .

— Esther Davis-Thompson

There is no doubt about how demanding raising inquisitive teens can be. Your every action is questioned and analyzed. It's hard work raising children, and it requires an extra layer of thoughtfulness, not to mention decisiveness.

Our kids often can't help themselves. It's how they are made up. They are often questioners at deep levels. As a parent you can work at being patient and clear with them. Even if you have moments when you feel like pulling your hair out, you can honor their questions. They are struggling to find their way, and your being there helps guide them.

Today I will respect my questioning teen for being the seeker he or she is.

October 25

Because teen sexual behavior today starts so much earlier than during our own coming of age, many parents find it hard to believe that it is as widespread as it really is. But parents can't afford to be complacent.

— Susan Panzarine

Is there a subject that's easier for most parents to avoid than sex? Yet the statistics on early sexual activity are alarming. It is happening more often and at younger ages. Kids need nuts-and-bolts information, and they need to know where you stand. They need information about what's good for them, what isn't, and concrete reasons why.

Good books exist on this topic; buying one for your child to read can lead to a good way to begin or enhance the conversation. A TV show that brings up the issue can be a good opening. So can an article in the newspaper. In general, the media can often provide ways for you to begin or focus on tricky conversations with your teen. Although it might make you feel anxious or ignorant, offering supportive information will help your child make healthy choices.

Part of my job as a parent is to educate my child about sexuality—there are books and other ways to help me do this.

October 26

What the world really needs is more love and less paperwork.

— Pearl Bailey

This statement makes me laugh; paperwork is such a universal complaint. Even my over-90-year-old aunt often complains about the stack of paperwork facing her. I think paperwork should be outlawed after ninety.

In the meantime, few things are more overwhelming than the stacks of paperwork that are a part of being human, and also a huge part of being a parent. There are medical forms, forms for school events, forms for extracurricular activities, forms for insurance. We all have to do it, but it's good to balance paperwork with a healthy dose of love. Paperwork tends to go more smoothly if it is balanced with love energy. When it's done, reward yourself.

Although paperwork is necessary, it is love that is really essential. Today I will take time from my paperwork to do one loving thing for myself or my child.

October 27

*Many influences contribute to our teenagers'
moral aspirations, including temperament,
level of energy, style, opportunities, and
challenges.*

— Right vs. Wrong: Raising
a Child with a Conscience

Preteens and teens care a lot about what their
friends think. Plus, they are living within a culture
that influences them in many ways. It's important as
parents to remember all the forces blowing around
them and to realize the small sliver of influence we
represent.

Although it helps to be aware of this reality, it
is also humbling. In a way we are turning our child
over to the universe. We can hope for and do all we
can to make it possible for teachers or coaches or
counselors or trusted adults within a faith community to be a positive influence. We can also encourage our teens to spend time with good friends, the
kind of friends who accept them and bring out the
best in them.

*Today I will be grateful for all the people who positively
care for and help shape my teenager's life.*

October 28

Create a family environment that encourages positive discussion about differences.

– What Kids Need to Succeed:
Proven, Practical Ways
to Raise Good Kids

Unfortunately, and all too often in the early teen years, it is the differences that are noticed and given a hard time. When I hear some of the putdowns that are used in school, I'm alarmed. Slurs are often about racial or sexual identity. As parents, we need to provide lessons to our teens about accepting differences.

Of course, this requires our own minds and hearts to be open. Our children are moving more and more into a culturally diverse world, and they need to be knowledgeable and accepting of this. We need to embrace and celebrate cultural and religious differences as well. If we see diversity as a rich and broadening part of life, we must consciously pass this on to our children.

I can celebrate the world's diversity, beginning right at my dinner table.

October 29

In the rush of daily living it's easy to forget all the remarkable people, real or fictional, who have been a part of your life. But if you just imagine they are near for a moment, you will realize that any one who ever touched your heart is always with you...whenever you remember to think of them.

-- Barbara Sher

Most of us remember a special relative or mentor who influenced us over the course of our lifetime—people who helped us, nourished us, strengthened us, deepened us. You can draw upon the wisdom and gifts of these people, for they live within you.

When you need courage in your parenting, re-member someone whose inspirational example you can emulate. If you need to lighten up, remember the wise one who always made you laugh. When you need patience, rely on what you learned from the loving patience shown by your role model. Spiri-tual warmth and support is available; we just need to seek it.

Today I will be conscious of a special kind of energy I need in my parenting and of a special person in my life I can emulate.

October 30

Nobody grows old merely by living a number of years. We grow old by deserting our ideals. Years wrinkle the skin, but to give up enthusiasm wrinkles the soul.

— Samuel Ullman

Sometimes we get so busy encouraging our children's interests and enthusiasms that we run out of time or money for our own. Since balance is a key to all true wisdom, it's important to keep our own inner flames alive. What is it that always lights you up? Is it biking, painting, writing poetry, windsurfing, weaving, fishing? The possibilities are endless.

Whether our enthusiasm is tried and true or an adventurous new one, feeding this fire has a way of feeding our youthful energy. To feel alive is to feel ageless. Alive is a good place to parent from.

I will do one thing today to feed a passion, an enthusiasm that is all mine.

October 31

It's Against the Law—Another source of
possible intervention is already in place. And
parents don't have to do a thing.

        ·- Dr. Anthony E. Wolf

One of the leverages in place for parents when it comes to drinking and other drug usage is the fact that both are illegal for teens. The same is true of breaking the curfew. Kids out after the curfew can and do get in trouble with the law. Kids found with alcohol in the car or on their bodies in the wrong place at the wrong time also get in trouble with the law.

As parents we need to use every advantage or piece of leverage we can find. Facts about legal repercussions can be useful. Sometimes we let this one slip by us, sliding into our teenagers' blasé ideas that they will never get caught. Kids do get caught. It is part of our job to remind our teens of this fact.

When I need to, I can take advantage of the fact that broken curfews and alcohol and other drug use are illegal and hold up this reality to my children.

November 1

*Our children are exposed to different chal-
lenges than we were as teens, . . . and they
solve problems differently than we would.*

⌐ Patty Wetterling

As I watch my older teen and all of her friends go
through the incredible challenge of looking at college choices, I realize what a different world she
lives in. In many ways, my choices were far simpler
when I was her age. Although I'm supportive in the
background, this is one of several areas where she is
forging her own problem-solving process. Thank
goodness for the college counselor at her high school,
and her friends, who share this journey with her.

My son, as a younger teen in an urban school, is
also faced with challenges that would have been unimaginable for me. The only way for me to understand their choices is to hear about and understand
some of their dilemmas.

*I will take time to appreciate how my child is navigat-
ing waters that are truly unfamiliar to me.*

November 2

Parents are the comforters.

— Doris Bodmer

Teens, and even preteens, navigate their way through school halls, romantic quandaries, academic challenges, and daily ups and downs. Where do they go to let their hair down? Even if you're negotiating delicate issues with your children, remember the ways they draw comfort from you and your home.

Perhaps it's the favorite meal you cook for them when they are celebrating an accomplishment or feeling down. Maybe it's how you allow them to just hunker down and relax once in a while. Sometimes you provide enormous comfort just by helping them with a project when they feel overwhelmed. My daughter could drive herself all over the city, but whenever she had a music audition I drove her. She always appreciated it, and I knew it was a small but tangible way to ease her nerves during a tense time.

Today I will keep my eyes open for an opportunity to comfort my child. All human beings can use a daily dose of comfort.

November 3

Kids have the capacity to like all kinds of music.

›- Tenessa Gemelke

Sometimes we underestimate our children in the music department. It's very easy to be close-minded about their musical tastes. But if we work a little bit at being open to "their" music, then we can begin the process of introducing some of "our" music to them. It's been fun to turn my heavy-metal son on to some rock-and-roll songs from his dad's and my era.

This kind of discussion requires a little extra effort and some conscious open-mindedness on the part of the adults. There is room for all kinds of musical tastes, and it's a wonderful thing to share with our kids.

Today I will give my kids the benefit of the doubt and ask them about their favorite kinds of music.

November 4

I am beginning to learn that it is the sweet, simple things of life which are the real ones after all.

·- Laura Ingalls Wilder

Your daughter comes home early one night and sits at the end of your bed, telling you all about her day. There's a sweetness to the moment, a deep appreciation of an enjoyable conversation. It nurtures a place deep inside you, one that is not often visited by your daughter who has a busy life and who focuses primarily on her friends and peers.

Moments like these come as unexpected gifts—simple moments of talking or laughter or a spontaneous outing, family rituals like Sunday evening dinners. These are the qualities of family life we miss when children go off to live their own lives. It is these moments that become touchstones for sharing and shared memories.

I will pay attention today to a sweet, simple moment that comes my way and appreciate it.

November 5

[I]f our aim is not to get caught up in lengthy battles, if our aim is to have them learn something positive, then . . . the greatest wisdom is simply to shut up.

— Dr. Anthony E. Wolf

Sometimes teenagers bring out the teenager inside of *us*. We revert to their level of maturity. An ongoing argument increases in volume and temperature, or a heated exchange encourages both sides to say things that shouldn't be said—never a pretty picture.

A friend has posted the maxim "Don't engage" on her refrigerator in bold, living color. Sometimes this means physically walking away. At other times it means biting one's tongue. Always it means restraint, holding steady in the storm. This will pass, and the outcome will be far more positive if we remember not to engage. Getting caught up in going-nowhere-fast battles will not teach our teens positive behaviors.

Today I will post the words "Don't engage" in a place where I most need to see them. In the heat of battle, wisdom lies in sometimes holding back.

November 6

*Our children cannot be open with us if we
impress them with how wrong they are.*

— Dr. Rudolph Dreikurs

Sometimes the words just slip out. "You're spoiled."
"You're lazy." "You're messing everything up." And
yet we all want our kids to be able to confide in us.
Pointing the finger and labeling their behavior is
rarely, if ever, constructive. We *can* let them know
how we feel about behavior that concerns us, and
all of this can be done without telling them they are
wrong or bad.

It's more challenging to listen than it is to judge,
and often, when those judging phrases pop up in
our minds, we need to refrain from saying them. It
never feels good to be on the receiving end of unconstructive criticism.

*Today I won't judge my child. I don't want to close the
door between us, I want to let it be open.*

November 7

*There is nothing wrong with allowing your
children to have a say in certain things about
their home life, but the laying of the home
foundation is a responsibility that a parent
cannot abdicate. . . .*

— Esther Davis-Thompson

The basic expectations and feeling of the home is
the parents' responsibility. Although we want our
children to be able to talk with us and to express
themselves, a home where the children have completely taken over, where there is very little control,
is a home on a shaky foundation.

As parents, we set the tone for a home that
feels safe and respectful for all, ourselves included.
We set the tone for a place that is friendly and wel-
comes others into it. We set the tone for a home
that includes gentleness and conversation.

*If my home feels out of control in any way, it is time to
remember that my job as parent is to lay and protect
this family's foundation.*

November 8

The patience and the humility of the face she loved so well was a better lesson to Jo than the wisest lecture, the sharpest reproof. She felt comforted at once by . . . the knowledge that her mother had a fault like hers, and tried to mend it. . . .

‑ Louisa May Alcott

Ahh, perfection. The desire to present ourselves as having it all figured out, of being perfectly in charge. Always.

The irony is that real connections with others often occur when we admit our own faults and weaknesses and talk honestly about the ways we cope with them. The day I tell my children just a bit about my own struggles with a bad temper, or with thinking I'm less worthy than those around me, is a day I build a bridge between us. It's also a chance to model and talk about how to cope, how to work with these weaknesses in a positive way.

I will be honest about my imperfections with my child when it's appropriate. I will remember that personal growth is possible and always ongoing.

November 9

A young person can never have too many supportive, trustworthy adults in his or her life.
 -- Kathleen Kimball-Baker

As parents we want to encourage healthy relationships for our teens with other adults. This might mean parents of their friends, coaches or teachers, or tutors or mentors. If we feel less popular or less beloved than these other people, we can practice having a generous heart. What we don't want to do is let our insecurities get in the way. As long as we can tell that the adult's relationship with our teen is a healthy one, one that helps her or him, it is best if we do all we can to encourage it.

A positive and upbeat attitude about the caring adults in our child's life is a way to be encouraging. So is thanking these special people or having them over for dinner.

I will do one thing today to honor or appreciate a special adult in my teen's life.

November 10

*Never be surprised by what is said in the car,
whether it be on a short trip to the grocery
store, on a long journey for summer vacation,
or in a typical Tuesday carpool.*

— Michael Riera

Car rides with your child are invaluable opportunities for hearing what's going on in his or her world. Rather than tuning in to the radio or your own preoccupations, tune in to your child. You are in a small box, contained for a period of time. Any issues simmering under the surface have a great chance of emerging.

Our first job is to be aware of this opportunity and our second job is quite simply to listen. It may or may not work to engage in conversation or ask questions—that's a judgment call to make based on the situation. But if your child needs a ride, or it's your turn to carpool, see it for what it is: an opportunity.

I will tune my listening ears and heart to my child's frequency today, especially in the car.

November 11

*Have room within your heart to hear the voice
of both your children and your own spirit.*

– William Martin

Here is the lifelong challenge of being a parent (and
I love the idea that this challenge requires room
within the heart): To offer our children a compassionate heart, an open heart, a loving heart. And
above all, a listening heart.

As parents, it's important to listen to our own
hearts: to be clear about what we need in order to
be good human beings and parents. A parent with a
clear, strong sense of self is a healthy parent. And it
is important to balance that sense of inner strength
with a heart that can open and stretch further to
listen to the inner, heartfelt voices of our teenagers.

*Today I will open my heart and listen—to myself and
to my child.*

November 12

It's easy to halve the potato where there's love.
~ Irish proverb

As parents we are called upon to share ourselves—
our time, energy, talents, finances, and more—in
many ways. Sometimes we may feel like we are running dry in any one or all of these areas. Yet deep
inside our hearts is a little furnace that keeps the
source of our energy alive—it's a glowing ember of
love. If that love feels frayed, sometimes all we need
is a short break: a night of sleep, an afternoon to
ourselves.

It's like keeping the furnace tuned up: old dust
wiped off makes way for the warm clean air. When
we can more clearly access our deep internal love
for our children, the giving comes more easily and
naturally.

Whatever I give my child today I will give in the spirit
of pure love.

November 13

Some family time should be set aside every week to enjoy each other's company . . . include your teen in the process of deciding how and when family time will be spent.

·~ Susan Panzarine

Even though kids may complain about family time cutting into their other plans, it also provides them a haven, a break from social pressures. Family time is a concrete way to feed the hearth-fire of family life. It lets our kids know they are important to us and it helps us remember who they are.

For some families it's dinnertime, for others it's a movie night or Sunday afternoon outing. Let your teen help plan the timing or the activity and she or he will be a more willing participant. These days it's easy for family time to disappear if it isn't scheduled. Family time is an essential way to both enjoy each other's company and check in with what's going on.

Family time is sacred time—I will keep a special place for it in our busy schedules.

November 14

What makes you worthwhile is who you are,
not what you do.

- Marianne Williams

From time to time we and our children can get caught up in comparing ourselves to others, and we fall short, of course. There will always be people around us winning awards, coming in first at something we wouldn't even attempt, making more money, driving a newer car, or getting a better part in the school play.

None of these things, in and of themselves, gives a person worth. It is who you are that really counts: Are you a loving family member? Are you honest? Are you a careful listener? Are you a good friend?

I will remember today that who I am, and who my child is, is what matters—not what we have done today.

November 15

Happy is he who learns to bear what he cannot change!

— Friederich Schiller

One of the more difficult experiences of parenting is when your child disappoints you. It's also painful to watch your child suffer in any way—physically, emotionally, academically. Your child has broken a leg at the height of her sports season, or your son has been involved in a school prank and is now in serious trouble at school. These scenarios, and many others, are difficult to witness.

Many of us have the tendency to play the "what if" mind game, expecting ourselves in hindsight to have foreseen and prevented what has happened. But what's done is done, and the sooner we move toward acceptance, as gracefully as we possibly can, the happier and more peaceful we can be inside ourselves. Once we make this shift, we can be more productive parents as we adjust and cope with how things are, rather than spinning our wheels wishing for things to be different.

Today I will find a way to gracefully bear the things I cannot change.

November 16

*Oh, to be only half as wonderful as my child
thought I was when he was small, and only
half as stupid as my teenager now thinks I am.*
— Rebecca Richards

Perhaps one of the biggest challenges as a parent is holding onto a sense of self through the many phases of the parenting experience. When our children are young, we bask in their sweet adoration. Later, with shock and grief, we realize how quickly our lofty positions can change—almost overnight. But even when our teens turn the flames of their disdain on us, we need to protect our inner core from the heat.

Sometimes all it takes is a friend to remind us we are no more stupid than we were when we were adored. Quiet time, reflection, and increasing our awareness of our inner strength can be helpful. Doing something we love and feeling the strength and wisdom of that experience coursing through our veins can help us stay strong for the next onslaught.

Today I will appreciate the person I know myself to be, whether or not my teenager agrees.

November 17

Show them how to cry / when pets and people die. . . .

-- William Martin

Pets are often very important in family life. They are a source of love for both parent and child and a bond that can often unite all members of a family. Other loving people in our lives also provide a uniting bond. These strands of love intertwine, creating a tapestry that adds beauty and strength to our lives and to our teens' lives as well.

Part of love is loss. When your grief over the loss of a special person or pet is shared with your child, your child learns an important lesson about love. The teen who learns to express her or his own grief is on the way to becoming a compassionate adult. The sharing of these feelings, in even the quietest of ways, creates a bond, a weaving upon the loom of love.

When loss knocks at our family door, we can share it.

November 18

You don't have to suffer to be a poet; adolescence is enough suffering for anyone.

·- John Ciardi

On the one hand, it seems like teenagers have more fun and more opportunities and more adventures than in previous eras. On the other hand, we need to remember that the teen years are still so much about sorting through one's identity, trying on different interests and ways of being, foraging through untravelled acres of friendships with both sexes, and grappling with a host of other complicated issues. All of this is stressful and demanding. It's not easy to find balance on this emotional seesaw.

It helps to take time once in a while to acknowledge all that your child is balancing. Empathy and compassion will go a long way toward meeting a child on common ground. Early teen years are especially ripe for tough kinds of learning.

When my child is crabby or seems to be having a bad day, I can first and foremost find compassion and empathy for all the issues he or she is navigating.

November 19

It is only by introducing the young to great literature, drama and music, and to the excitement of great science that we open to them the possibilities that lie within the human spirit—enable them to see visions and dream dreams.

.~ Eric Anderson

Education, learning, reading, exposure to the arts—these are all assets for our children. They are assets not just because they can help our teens earn good grades or get into college but because they contain deep truths of the human spirit. Certainly, stories that have been read and studied for hundreds of years can teach a great deal about the longings, loyalties, and imperfections of human beings.

Drama often holds up a mirror to life, even for skeptical teenagers. And music of all kinds holds the potential to soothe and uplift us. As parents, we can encourage our children in their education by being interested in what they are learning and by making learning of all kinds accessible to them.

Today I will look for an opportunity to encourage an open heart and mind today in my teenager—open to all there is to be learned, absorbed, and celebrated in this world.

November 20

Normal day, let me be aware of the treasure
you are.

— Mary Jean Irion

Days without a major sickness or a major crisis are
days that fall into this category. Such days may contain mild irritations or the usual demands of a busy
life raising teenagers. These are the days that, gathered together, form the blur of ordinary time, days
and days of it.

What we often forget to do is appreciate the
normal days. In a similar way, good health is often
appreciated only immediately after being sick, or
in contrast to being sick. Appreciation of a normal
day usually intensifies when a crisis appears on the
scene. But we don't need to wait for that. We can
appreciate the beauty and contentment possible in
every normal day we receive.

Today I will appreciate fully every bit of my life that is
going well in its quiet, ordinary, normal way.

November 21

We worry about what a child will be tomorrow, yet we forget that he is someone today.
— Stacia Tauscher

As parents we have a tendency to worry about the future. We worry about what road a child might head down. We worry about college. We worry about what they will be when they grow up. We worry about the potential bad influence of a new friend.

All children need to know their parents see them as capable and lovable today. Each child has unique strengths and talents. Rather than notice what they *aren't* doing, we can pay attention to where they *are* applying their talents and skills. Some days we may have to look harder than other days. But it's worth the effort—for our sake and for the sake of our children.

Today I will notice something in particular that makes my teen somebody special, somebody who matters today.

November 22

*If our children are to approve of themselves,
they must see that we approve of ourselves.*

·-- Maya Angelou

Over and over again, the work of parenting is two-fold: to take care of ourselves and to take care of our children. This is especially true when our children are passing through the teen years. Often we get so focused on taking good care of them and on being good parents that we forget the other part of this equation.

If we want them to have good self-esteem, we must model having it ourselves. If we want them to communicate well and with respect, we must do it ourselves. If we want them to learn to love and like themselves, we teach this best by liking and loving ourselves.

*Today I will do whatever it takes to approve of myself,
for my own sake and for what I want to teach my child.*

November 23

The trees in your orchard . . . the flocks in your pastures . . . give that they may live, for to withhold is to perish.

— Kahlil Gibran

Open hearts don't come easily in this world. Somewhere along the way our hearts perhaps have been wounded or frightened. So we hold back—we hold back affection, we hold back on candidness or spontaneity, we hold back on compliments or admiration, we hold back our questions.

Yet a life of withholding is a life that is far closer to perishing than thriving. And so, it is good to pay attention to where we withhold and to invite ourselves out of that cocoon. It's not so hard—it just requires awareness. And with practice it becomes much easier.

If I feel an impulse to withhold a compliment or a gesture I will let it out today. My heart is growing, blooming, overflowing, and ready for expression.

November 24

The right man comes at the right time.

·- Italian proverb

So much of the intuitive work of parenting relies on a sense of timing. Discipline, well-timed, is more constructive than if it comes at a less fruitful time. And a moment, the right moment, seized for celebration, may not come again for a long time. Such moments bond you and your child in special ways.

There are times when the best thing you can do is make your child take the next step. And there are times when the best thing you can do is accept that your child has done her or his best, for the moment. Just like weddings are for dancing and funerals are for weeping, so are there times to step in and times to step back as a parent.

As a parent I will listen closely to myself and my child— what is it time to embrace today?

November 25

Mothers go on getting blamed until they're 80,
but shouldn't take it personally.

·- Katharine Whitehorn

I sometimes wonder if there is any harder challenge to the ego in this world than parenting. The expectations are huge, and the "falling short" is not accepted by ourselves or by those around us very gracefully.

Friends are invaluable in this department. It can be hard not to take our teenagers' disdain, judgment, or criticism personally. Very hard indeed, especially when we are at the receiving end so often.

I will talk or walk with a friend today who will remind
me to not take my teen's slights personally. I will remind
every parent I talk to today of the same resolution.

November 26

*Live your life each day as you would climb
a mountain. An occasional glance toward the
summit keeps the goal in mind, but many
beautiful scenes are to be observed from each
new vantage point.*

~ Harold B. Melchart

Raising children is like a long climb, especially in the teen years. You want to keep your eyes on the summit. The outcomes you're striving for might relate to raising loving children who develop their talents and treat others well along the way. But in the midst of the bumpy, sometimes circuitous journey are amazing moments to linger over and appreciate.

A return to the daily climb may bring you to surprising and beautiful panoramas along the way, followed by more steps forward. Each stage in your child's life offers moments to savor and reflect upon how far you both have come. Enjoy those moments, as well as the slow, steady progress that brings you to them.

Today I will savor the climb and the view from this beautiful, challenging mountain of parenthood.

November 27

Reading is to the mind what exercise is to the body.

- Joseph Addison

Part of what makes a young teen healthy and confident is a deep interest in learning. This can come in many forms, but it is something we parents should model and encourage. Books and musical lessons stretch and strengthen the brain like physical exercise does the body.

Access to books is a gift we can give to our teenagers. A reading corner or a place to study are ways we tell them that we honor who they are as learners. Teens can be especially excited when we sometimes read and enjoy the same books!

Today I will honor one way my teen is learning about our world: I will ask about a book he is reading, or share one with him.

November 28

I get by with a little help from my friends.
                                            – The Beatles

My daughter and her friends formed a tight study group during their high school years. They quizzed each other, explained math solutions to each other, analyzed poems together. They took study breaks together—alternating hard work with easy laughter. I loved watching this.

When my own friend's father died, several of us called and sent flowers. We checked on her often and closely in the following weeks. When another friend was hospitalized, we all pitched in and brought meals for a month. In a million different ways, friendship makes the world a kinder and gentler place.

Where can I be a good friend today and encourage my teen to do the same?

November 29

It is an illusion to think that more comfort means more happiness. Happiness comes of the capacity to feel deeply, to enjoy simply, to think freely, to risk life, to be needed.

— Storm Jameson

The capacity to feel deeply and enjoy the simple things in life: that this deep appreciation is connected to the fundamental ability to feel happy is an important life connection we want our teens to grasp. Teens are notorious for wanting more things. Shopping malls can be magnets, leading teens to think they would be happier if only they had a car or more expensive clothes.

We all want our children to be happy, and as adults we can get sidetracked into thinking if we only had one more thing we would be happier. So, to keep ourselves planted and to help plant the possibility of happiness in our teenagers, we need to remember: Happiness is about how we approach life, not what we have. Happiness comes from knowing we are needed and appreciated.

Today I will encourage in myself and my teen the ability to appreciate the world beyond material possessions.

November 30

Gratitude is a sometime thing in this world. Just because you've been feeding them all winter, don't expect the birds to take it easy on your grass seed.

~ Bill Vaughan

There is no way children can or will appreciate in their youth what parents do for them—the many financial drains, how much they demand of our time and energy. Parenting involves a lot of giving, and it is just about impossible for teenagers to grasp the extent of this effort on their behalf. If we expect them to understand, we will be banging our heads against that familiar brick wall.

I do sometimes remind my teen to thank me; this is an important "people skill." But this is different from insisting our teens owe us something in return for all we give them. The birds we feed are preparing to fly out of the nest: we nurture their wings, without sending a bill for services rendered.

I feed my children from a deep well because I love them, not because of anything I expect in return.

December 1

Blessed is the season which engages the whole world in a conspiracy of love.

— Hamilton Wright Mabie

The heart of winter is a time when many people celebrate. Some honor the winter solstice, others celebrate Christmas. Jewish people light candles for Hanukkah and African-Americans celebrate family time during Kwanzaa. It is striking that so many traditions at this time of year incorporate rituals of lighting candles in the midst of the darkness.

What these special events all have in common is that they are times for honoring family by gathering together for special meals or rituals. It's about love, it's about being together, and it's about honoring our spiritual lives together. The need for togetherness is universal.

In small and simple ways, I will honor this time as a family time, as a time to celebrate the love we have for each other.

December 2

[A]s teenagers, they are out in the real world—
a world that has real dangers. This we have
to accept. We cannot hold them back.
— Dr. Anthony E. Wolf

This is one of the more painful realities of navigating the teen years. To a great extent, what we have given our children up to this point is what will sustain them out in the world. They will need every shred of strength, awareness, and sense of self they have developed. For they are navigating waters full of promise but are also surrounded by drugs, alcohol, sexual issues, pressures from other kids, and, above all, a cultural bias toward "coolness."

Unless we lock them in their rooms for their teen years, our children have to learn to grapple on their own with the hazards and challenges of their world. Accepting this reality is an important aspect of parenting children in this age group. We can love them, support them, and expect the best from them. Cope with their mistakes, love them again. But we cannot really hold them back from the world. It is their necessary journey to adulthood.

Letting go is part of my job right now. Sometimes I just need to let my teen set sail so he can learn his own lessons.

December 3

*So for the moment I maintain my balance . . .
by vigilant and conscious monitoring of my
needs along with those of my kids. It is a necessary habit.*

— Mary Guerrera Congo

Nothing is more demanding in the caretaking department than parenting. Parenting teens, although
less physically hands-on than parenting toddlers, can
be an enormous challenge, emotionally and mentally.

What often weakens our ability to deal with our
kids clearly and fairly is stress and fatigue. When we
shortchange our own needs for relaxation, friendship, and self-renewal, we shortchange our ability to
be whole and wholesome parents.

*I will write down three ways I can take care of myself,
today and in the next few days. I will promise to make
them a priority.*

December 4

*Work on accepting [your child's] right to be
who they are and to think what they think,
just as you want them to accept your right to
be who you are and to think what you think.*

— Janet Woititz

Most of us know what it feels like when our teenager curls her lip in disdain, or when he lets us know just how stupid he thinks we are. It never feels good, even if we understand that being seen in such a way is not so unusual. Likewise, when we are sharp or critical with our children, it never feels good to them. If we second-guess their decisions, or judge them for the way they think or act, we bring them down.

Accepting differences between people is important in all aspects of life and needs to begin at home. If we primarily love, respect, and admire our children—in spite of occasionally disagreeing with them—then there's a chance for us to mutually enjoy and admire each other.

Today I will work on accepting my teenager in the same way I want her or him to accept me.

December 5

There is more to life than increasing its speed.
                                   — Mohandas K. Gandhi

Most of the parents I know spend a lot of time driving, a lot of time juggling their kids' many activities. It seems to be the modern way. The hurried pace makes for frenetic souls and bad tempers. It also leaves little time for easy conversation or gestures of affection and gratitude.

Our culture's busyness is so widespread and so mainstream that it takes effort to honor the opposite: unscheduled time, a slower pace. Yet knowing that it's okay to relax is an essential part of being a fully alive human being.

When I see the opportunity, I will save space in our family life for an evening or afternoon of relaxation. It's good for our spirits.

December 6

Too many people miss the silver lining because they're expecting gold.

— Maurice Setter

Sometimes we look for certain standards in our children, or involvement in a particular event or activity. When what they want differs from what we want, it's easy to be disappointed. But so what if, instead of soccer, she decides to do swimming? Or he gets a B+ in math instead of his usual straight As?

There are many mild complaints like these in the world of parenting. When they surface, we can resolve to widen and deepen our perspective. Silver linings can become apparent if we don't have our hearts set on too-defined or narrow a streak of gold.

Let me notice the silver lining in my teen's life today.

December 7

Change starts when someone sees the next step.
― William Drayton

Sometimes there are situations in a family that need change. One child is acting out rebelliously and making life difficult for all. Or a parent is particularly stressed about a job-related issue and creating an irritable atmosphere at home.

Denial or lack of awareness can lengthen these difficult periods. And then one day the desire for change emerges. Although complete solutions are not always readily apparent or simple, if one just knows the next step to take, change is set in motion. Perhaps it's a phone call or a heart-to-heart conversation. One step at a time paves the way forward.

I will be grateful today for knowing what the next simple step is that I need to take as a parent.

December 8

If we are to truly be guides for our children,
we need to "go fishing" in their lives, often.
— Esther Davis-Thompson

Fishing requires casting a line into the water and
seeing what's there, hiding beneath the surface. Some
days there's nothing biting, other days we get only
subtle nibbles, and some days there are large and
small fishing jumping onto the end of that line, tugging it at insistently.

The calm surface of our teens' exteriors can belie
what is going on beneath. As parents we can take
the time to go fishing, to hang the line of a question or easy conversation starter over the edge of
our day into their waters, their interests, their days'
events. Some days, nothing will bite. But keep fishing, because some days there's a lot of story to be
caught and pulled to the surface.

Today I will take time to go fishing for conversation and
story in my teen's world.

December 9

> . . . [T]eenagers need to extend away from
> their parents, all the while staying connected
> to their parents. Their job is to extend; your
> job is to connect.
>
> — Michael Riera

When my teen is overtired or sick, she is far more
vulnerable than usual. I like to be there during these
times. It seems like an opportunity, and an especially
tender one at that, to feed the connection between
us. Tender moments are few and far between, but
they are felt, I believe, by both of us at a deep level.

Rare are the moments when she is so open
and in need of my empathy. Rare are the moments
when she lets me comfort her. Rare are the moments when I get to remember and see and care for
the child within her. Within days she will be busily
extending away from me again, back to her work.

Although I would never wish for my child's vulnerable
moments, I can use them as a way to make a special
connection.

December 10

One day He / tipped His top hat / and walked / out of the room, / ending the argument.

.- Anne Sexton

One friend whose daughter was going through a tumultuous and moody time found that her daughter often started arguments for no reason. These arguments never solved anything and usually escalated the level of anger and resentment between them.

My friend discovered that if she zipped her lip or walked away when her daughter was trying to provoke a confrontation, it helped to defuse the situation. This made it easier to talk to her daughter later, when the heat of the moment had subsided.

The next time my son or daughter tries to argue with me, I will stay strong, remain calm, and save the discussion for later.

December 11

Music washes away from the soul the dust of everyday life.

·-- Berthold Auerbach

Music can offer a great venue for sharing between parents and teens. Although it is easy to misunderstand some of their music, and certainly we don't have to like it all, it's good to make the most of any musical connection you discover. It's even worth looking proactively for such connections.

A friend's son loves drumming and listens to music that mystifies his parents. His dad found a Led Zeppelin drum solo (Dad's era of music) and shared it with his son. This act began a sharing of drum solos that each of them found, and the father took a teeny, tiny step toward being "cool" or perhaps, more accurately, accessible to his teen.

I can look for ways that music can be a source of connection with my teen—even something as simple as enjoying the same song on the radio in the car.

December 12

When young people can spend time with special aunts and uncles [or cousins], the whole family benefits.

— Kathleen Kimball-Baker

Family relationships build quietly with time spent together during holidays, birthdays, reunions, or other special gatherings. In my own life, two aunts and an uncle were important sources of love for me. When things were good with my parents, my aunts and uncle supplied an abundance of care. When things were rocky with my parents, my relatives provided an unwavering and unconditional source of love that always sustained me.

We can foster and nurture extended family relationships by asking a family member to spend special time with our teens. Most people are honored to be asked. We can invite special family members over for dinner as a way to keep those relationships strong. Doing these things will help build bridges— bridges to share in times of fun and celebration, and bridges that provide a safe crossing in times of trouble and need.

What can I do to invite more family support into my teen's life?

December 13

From the day your baby is born, you are a teacher of spirit. If you create an atmosphere of trust, openness, non-judgment and acceptance, those qualities will be absorbed as the qualities of spirit.

꙳ Deepak Chopra

Trusting openness may come more easily when your child is five years old. And if you spend a moment thinking about the opposite of the qualities listed by Chopra, words like *fear, judgment,* and *rejection* come to mind. Most of us do not want to raise our kids in an atmosphere of fear, suspicion, rejection, distrust. And yet, as they enter and sail through the teen years, from time to time we will dip our fingers and toes into the edge of all of these negative pools.

But we can always pull ourselves back to the shore of expecting the best of our kids. Trust can be rebuilt and is worth rebuilding. Openness to who our children really are requires an ongoing opening of our parental hearts. The spiritual essence of home is knit with emotional threads, and we want to keep weaving in the threads of open acceptance, of trust.

I will pay attention to my teen's and my spiritual lives today, working to replace fear with acceptance.

December 14

*Sometimes the best helping hand you can
give is a good, firm push.*

·– Joann Thomas

Indecisiveness plagues us all, whether adult or teen,
from time to time. The inability to make the next
move can be paralyzing. Although there are periods
in our lives when waiting is the wisest thing to do,
at some point it is best to take action.

The action that is daunting, difficult, or demanding is one we need a push to make. Is your teen in
need of a push to get a job, try out for a new activity,
or stop dating the person who makes her feel so
bad? When we harness our parenting intuition and
the need for action becomes clear, it's worth stretching ourselves as parents to lovingly push our fledg-
lings out of the nest and into flight.

*Where might I need to give my teen a boost toward
action? When I see the need, I can garner my own resources to help me make the push—firmly, lovingly.*

December 15

Teasing, like laughter, can build esteem and encourage intimacy, or it can cruelly discount.

— Growing Up Again:
Parenting Ourselves,
Parenting Our Children

How is humor used in your family? What do you model about humor as a parent? Humor, well-used, can be a way to share laughter, to share intimate jokes, to enjoy life's absurdities together. A lot of love and tenderness can be embedded in a nickname or in gentle teasing.

Yet teasing and humor can also easily slide into a putdown, whether subtle or overt. It can also be used as a disguise for anger. As a parent you want to be vigilant about this kind of teasing. It is neither direct nor helpful. It often hurts the recipient. The dagger of anger, no matter how it is disguised, is still felt in a way that is confusing and unconstructive.

I will pay attention to my teasing and humor, highlighting it when it's loving and discarding it when its underlying motive is anger or meanness.

December 16

Celebrate when your child acts on a belief or conviction, especially when it was obviously hard to do.

— What Kids Need to Succeed:
Proven, Practical Ways
to Raise Good Kids

Your child tells you of a kind gesture he made to someone who was being picked on at lunch. You hear from a teacher that your daughter was kind to the new girl when no one else was. You find out your child spoke up to her friends about the destructive effects of drug abuse she witnessed in a relative recently, making it clear she doesn't think it's cool.

There are many ways our children may step out on a limb and act on behalf of their compassion or political beliefs. It's never easy to stand up alone and make a statement. When you hear of your child doing this, celebrate and honor the clarity and courage such an action took. Let them know how much you admire what they did.

I will take time to celebrate moments of belief and conviction in my child.

December 17

When you do stumble upon the magic question that sparks a connection, file that information away for later use.

– Tenessa Gemelke

It can be hard to engage some kids in conversation. Whether we are trying to converse with our own kids or with their friends, it really does pay to keep trying. Sometimes it takes a few attempts to get to a question a child really cares about. Take a break if you feel like you're getting nowhere, but don't give up. Somewhere inside of everybody is a topic that excites them. Keep digging. It's worth the effort it takes to find it.

Once you do, remember it and pull it out again. Most stories have updates over time. If your son is wild about a certain music group, that's worth several questions. You could ask about the songs, their touring schedule, the names of their CDs, or their band members. When a child lights up and wants to talk you've done good work. Keep it up.

Today I will look for the right question to ask my children and their friends.

December 18

*By sending love, compassion, and kindness
to confront the problems of anger, resentment,
and bitterness . . . they simply dematerialize.*
                                                    ·~ Wayne Dyer

As a parent we will run into anger and resentment and bitterness in our children. We may also find these negative feelings erupting in ourselves. They are human, never pretty, and feel restless and disruptive, whether at the giving or receiving end.

Do we want our kids to look back on our time together as a primarily positive or negative experience? With that question in mind, it is fruitful to challenge ourselves to dig a level deeper and find love, compassion, and kindness within ourselves. First, we need to look within our own hearts and minds, and then into the hearts and minds of our teenagers.

Today I will be wise enough to replace anger with love, resentment with compassion, and bitterness with kindness.

December 19

That man is a success who has lived well,
laughed often and loved much. . . .

～ Robert Louis Stevenson

Although living well means different things to different people, laughing often and loving much are easier concepts to grasp clearly. Ideally, don't we all want our children to remember a home where people laughed easily and felt very loved? One wonders why these simple concepts are so easy to forget in the humdrum of daily obligations.

To laugh often and love much demands a consciousness from most of us. Openness to loving often requires simple gesture—an open heart, rather than one closed with worries. Laughter flows more easily out of a relaxed sense about life. Hurry and laughter rarely go together.

I will take time today for easy laughter and gestures of love.

December 20

The true picture of life as it is, if it could be adequately painted, would show men what they are, and how they might rise, not, indeed to perfection, but one step first, and then another on the ladder.

·~ Anthony Trollope

The importance of focusing on progress rather than perfection is an idea we all need to be reminded of. It's a concept that is simple, direct, and all too often forgotten. Yet it is a crucial lifeline that can keep us from sinking under the weight of our own demands for perfection.

As caretakers we often feel the need to "fix" things, to solve problems, to wrap up a project and call it done. But some tasks aren't finished so quickly and neatly. That tendency of our teens to be mean when under pressure, that quick-to-yell impulse when we, the adults, are overtired? These are for-the-long-haul projects. On this road of life, steps backward have to be accepted (and sometimes forgiven), and steps forward acknowledged.

If I'm feeling discouraged, I will sit down and list the progress, the small positive steps both my child and I have made.

December 21

Books may well be the only true magic.
       -- Alice Hoffman

Sharing books with a teen can be a rich and rewarding experience for both of you. If you know what your teen is reading for English, pick it up for yourself and talk about it with your child. Talking about books is a great way to get to know your child as a learner and as a thinker. It's also a great way to get to know your child's values.

Books and learning of all sorts open teens to the world around them. As parents, we ideally want to be fellow explorers with our teens as they begin to venture out into the unknown. One important way to do this is to take an interest in what they are learning.

Today I will remember that the magic of books is something I can share with my teen.

December 22

*Marijuana gave me wings, but took away
the sky.*

.– Anonymous

You could replace the word "marijuana" with any
drug substance. In the beginning it feels good. Getting high or being intoxicated tends to make people
feel expansive. Expansive, but no longer able to drive
home safely. Expansive, but unable to focus on the
task at hand.

How do we teach our children that if they use alcohol, tobacco, or other drug substances, their usage
can limit and narrow their world? How do we let
them know that substance abuse among adolescents
has consequences some people never recover from?
We can borrow the words of Anonymous, written
by someone who has lived the experience. Notice the
acknowledgment and the pain buried within those
few words.

*I will share what I know of the dangers of alcohol or
other drug use—my child deserves this information.*

December 23

> [T]o leave the world a bit better, whether by
> a healthy child, a garden patch or a redeemed
> social condition; to know even one life has
> breathed easier because you have lived. This
> is to have succeeded.
>
> ⁓ Ralph Waldo Emerson

Most of us live fairly ordinary lives, and the daily repetition of parenting can contribute to this feeling of ordinariness. The idea of success is nebulous and is often easier to see in others than to feel in oneself. And yet, in the wise and transcendental words of Emerson, the simple daily job of raising an emotionally healthy child is indeed a valuable contribution.

There are other simple ways of making the world a better place. Do a kind deed for your neighbor and have your child help you do it. Plant a garden by yourself or with your child; enjoy its harvests with your family and your neighbors. The successes you have in raising your child are often quiet ones, but day after day they gain a profound power and strength that are true contributions to this world.

I can honor my successes as a parent: they are quiet but powerful, subtle but deeply felt.

December 24

More than they ever let on, most teens want to please their parents.

⁓ John Freeman

It's so easy to forget that our children want to please us, even though somewhere in our hearts we know this is true. No one lets us know in a quicker or sharper way what is wrong with us than our teenage children. How could they possibly want to please someone they seem to scorn so much?

Beneath the contempt is the deep connection between parent and child, the bond they must break free from during these years so that they can grow into independent adults. The effort put into breaking free speaks to the power of the bond. And always, even as they find ways to push us away, they still need not only our presence, but also our acceptance and even approval.

I will take a moment today to trust that my teen wants to please me; I will let her or him know one concrete way that I appreciate her or him.

December 25

God gave burdens, also shoulders.

– Yiddish proverb

Most of us struggle with something: for some of us it's earning enough money to pay our bills; for another it's a family member's addiction; for another it's helping a child cope with a learning disability or depression; for some it might be chronic illness. Even those who look like they lead perfect lives have struggles and burdens that are only known to those closest to them.

What we have in common is the need to cry or rest on another's shoulders. All of us need the comfort, support, and empathy of others at times. And we all need the strength of our own shoulders as well. We are stronger than we knew before we were tested. We can both carry the weight of our burdens and share it with others who care.

As heavy as my problems feel, I have ample strength and supportive help to face them.

December 26

Can you encourage your children without attaching too much importance to the outcome?
~ William Martin

One of the hazards of parenting is becoming overly invested in who our children are and what they become. A key to look for within this puzzle is: Do we need them to be or do something in order for us to feel good about who *we* are?

Many of us provide lessons and opportunities for our children; we make numerous sacrifices for them in this regard. We know it's important to encourage their talents and skills, and we need to remember that for them, as well as for us, this life is about the journey. The tennis lessons allow a teen to develop skills and love the game itself. Toward that process, rather than to winning the championship game and the inherent glory, is where we need to direct our encouragement.

Today I will cheer my child on without focusing on any grand outcome.

December 27

*. . . [T]rust is . . . very difficult to build and
very easy to destroy.*

·– Thomas J. Watson Sr.

Trust is a word that is used and abused. How often
do children throw out, "You don't trust me," as a way
of making us change our minds or shift our boundaries? When teens employ this tactic, it's best to veer
away from the issue of trust altogether. Boundaries
are boundaries, and they exist because of our own
considered limits and rules, separate from the issue
of trust.

Trust is about honesty and respect for each other
and the rules. When this trust is broken it needs to
be discussed. A loss of trust usually warrants a loss
of privileges. It can be broken in the space of one evening, but it can only be genuinely rebuilt over time.
Children deserve to hear about this: it's a lesson that
will apply to relationships for the rest of their lives.

*Today I will be honest about the issue of trust between
my child and me—how it gets built, and how it might
be broken.*

December 28

Our best refuge is to have confidence in our children and to take it easy until such time as our talents for coping with disaster are really called upon.

– Dr. Rudolph Dreikurs

Worry is a feeling that easily haunts a parent's repertoire. There are so many areas to worry about: classes, friends, activities, energy levels. Many of us confuse our responsibility as a parent with a need to worry. Many of us imagine difficulties and troubles where none have yet appeared.

Unless and until our children prove themselves to be unworthy of our trust, it is best to be confident in them. Believe they are in good shape and able to make good choices and impart this belief to them. Confidence and a positive outlook toward our teens will help foster positive results.

Where there is no need, I will throw worry out my window. Instead, I will express confidence in my teen's ability and desire to make good choices.

December 29

We love those people who give with humility,
or who accept with ease.

— Freya Stark

The world of parenting, when it's working well, can be ripe with opportunities for giving and receiving. Between parent and child. Between parent and other parents. Between families. Think of the times a carpool has saved you or someone you know. Remember the organized meal plan for a family in medical crisis. Honor the life experience a child had while traveling with a friend's family.

The most loving and clear giving happens in a spirit of humility, not grandiosity, without a sense of anything being owed in return. The most light-filled way to receive is with appreciation, gratitude, an open heart. Often we have to step over pride or self-consciousness to be good givers and receivers.

Today I will give where I can, knowing I am fortunate to be able to give, and I will receive what comes to me with the ease of an open and grateful heart.

December 30

Gratitude is the memory of the heart.

— Jean Baptiste Massieu

At year's end we are often inspired to consider our goals for the year ahead. It's a good time to reflect on goals, highlights, and needs along this remarkable life journey. It's also a great time to consciously practice gratitude.

In sweeping your eyes and hearts over the previous year, what are the moments, events, and gifts you feel grateful for—in your individual life, your family life, your child's life? Honor those moments with your attention, and your heart will light up like a shoreline greeting the rising sun. Gratitude bathes experience in a warm and golden light.

Today I will remember and feel warmed by the gifts of this past year. I enter the new year remembering how blessed I am.

December 31

In three words I can sum up everything I've learned about life: It goes on.

– Robert Frost

After an eventful moment in one's life, whether it's a loss or achievement, it can seem surprising that life just goes on. Your mother dies, but your neighbor still goes out the door to buy groceries. You just received a huge promotion at work, but your teenager still isn't speaking to you.

This "going-on-ness" can seem strange or disappointing at times. But it can also be comforting. The sun rises every morning and we get to begin again, to do all those things that demand doing day after day. We get a chance to be alive again.

The way that life goes on can be a source of comfort and inspiration for me today.

Additional Search Institute Resources

"Ask Me Where I'm Going" & Other Revealing Messages from Today's Teens. This small, intimate book will touch your heart with its poignant and practical "real words" from teens describing what they want from the caring adults in their lives.

Connect 5: Finding the Caring Adults You May Not Realize Your Teen Needs by Kathleen Kimball-Baker. Parents don't have to be all things at all times to their teens. Many teens yearn for more warm, trusting relationships with caring adults. In *Connect 5*, author (and mother) Kathleen Kimball-Baker provides hope, encouragement, and practical advice for parents in reaching out and helping their teens connect with other responsible and supportive adults, a critical factor in teens' healthy development.

Conversations on the Go: Clever Questions to Keep Teens and Grown-Ups Talking by Mary Ackerman. This stimulating, go-anywhere book gives teens and adults a chance to find out what each other really thinks. Filled with intriguing questions, some deep and some just fun, this book is guaranteed to stretch the imagination and bring out each person's personality and true self.

Parenting at the Speed of Teens: Positive Tips on Everyday Issues. Parenting at the Speed of Teens is a practical, easy-to-use guide that offers positive, commonsense strategies for dealing with the everyday issues of parenting teenagers—junk food, the Internet, stress, jobs, friends—as well as serious issues teens may also encounter—depression, divorce, racism, substance abuse. It illustrates how the daily "little things" such as talking one-on-one, setting boundaries, offering guidance, and modeling positive behavior make a big difference in helping a teenager become successful during these challenging, exciting adolescent years. The book is written around common parent issues, questions, and frustrations. Parents will relate to the real-life dilemmas addressed in chapters on Home and Family, School, Friends and Peers, Work, Image, and Special Issues. Parents will find comfort and reassurance in the assets-based parenting perspective and advice.

Who, Me? Surprisingly Doable Ways You Can Make a Difference for Kids. Use this desktop perpetual calendar for reminders, tips, and inspiration in your daily interactions with kids and teens. Here you'll find great, concrete asset-building ideas from dozens of the best Search Institute youth publications.

WHY Do They Act That Way? A Survival Guide to the Adolescent Brain for You and Your Teen by David Walsh, Ph.D., with Nat Bennett. Even smart kids do stupid things. It's a simple fact of life. No one makes it through the teenage years unscathed—not the teens and not their parents. But now there's expert help for both generations in this groundbreaking new guide for surviving the drama of adolescence. In *WHY Do They Act That Way?*, National Institute on Media and the Family's president and award-winning psychologist, Dr. David Walsh, explains exactly what happens to the human brain on the path from childhood to adolescence and adulthood. Revealing the latest scientific findings in easy-to-understand terms, Dr. Walsh shows why moodiness, quickness to anger and take risks, miscommunication, fatigue, territoriality, and other familiar teenage behavior problems are so common—all are linked to physical changes and growth in the adolescent brain. *Published by Free Press.*

MVPARENTS

MVParents—Online and other resources developed by Search Institute specifically for busy, caring parents who want information they can trust about raising responsible children and teens. For more information, visit MVParents.com.

About the Author

Patricia Hoolihan holds an M.A. in Creative Writing from the University of Minnesota. Her books include *Small Miracles: Daily Meditations for Mothers in Recovery* and *Teen Girls Only: Daily Thoughts for Teenage Girls*. She has published essays in the *Walker Art Center Catalog, Flight Training Magazine* and online in *Milkweed Editions*. A chapter of her memoir was published in *Water Stone* and won Honorable Mention for the Brenda Ueland Prose Prize. Another chapter of her memoir was published in *Great River Review* and won first place in the Writers on Time Competition. She teaches a variety of writing classes at The Loft Literary Center and at Metropolitan State University, both in Minneapolis.

About Search Institute Press

Search Institute Press is a division of Search Institute, a nonprofit organization that offers leadership, knowledge, and resources to promote positive youth development. Our mission at Search Institute Press is to provide practical and hope-filled resources to help create a world in which all young people thrive. Our products are embedded in research, and the 40 Developmental Assets®—qualities, experiences, and relationships youth need to succeed—are a central focus of our resources. Our logo, the SIP flower, is a symbol of the thriving and healthy growth young people experience when they have an abundance of assets in their lives.